ALBERT A. VERMEULEN

# Corporate Success

## A Fresh Focus on Strategy

iUniverse, Inc.
Bloomington

Corporate Success
A Fresh Focus on Strategy

iUniverse books may be ordered through booksellers or by contacting:

iUniverse
1663 Liberty Drive
Bloomington, IN 47403
www.iuniverse.com
1-800-Authors (1-800-288-4677)

ISBN: 978-1-4620-3874-9 (sc)
ISBN: 978-1-4620-3875-6 (hc)
ISBN: 978-1-4620-3876-3 (e)

Library of Congress Control Number: 2011912853

Printed in the United States of America

iUniverse rev. date: 9/28/2011

To Janettha, Nicolaas, and Aletta

# Contents

# List of Illustrations/Tables

# Preface

Organizations struggle to design and implement strategies to the point where the strategies deliver the intended results. At the beginning of my career, I experienced firsthand the challenges large organizations in South Africa faced as they wrestled to adjust their strategies to accommodate changes in the political and economic landscapes. Later, as a senior executive, I had to address similar challenges. How could my team and I design and implement a strategy that would secure the intended results? I couldn't find a practical solution. I studied the reasons strategies fail, observed the behaviors of employees and leaders during the design and implementation of strategies, talked to thousands of employees and leaders, and launched several exploratory-designed experiments to validate my observations. I concluded that a change-enabling milieu, in combination with three critical connections—psychological, structural, and contractual—secure the adoption of a new strategy and significantly elevate the odds that a strategy will deliver the intended results.

As my consulting career unfolded as president of Arrowhead Management & Associates LLC, a consulting firm that specializes in driving the adoption of corporate strategies in collaboration with organizational leaders, I supported organizations in the implementations of their strategies. I capitalized on those opportunities and refined my approach to strategy design and implementation to the level where organizations achieve highly successful and sustainable results. I share my practical approach to design and implement a strategy with those leaders and organizations that want results.

# Acknowledgments

I would like to acknowledge my mentor, Karen Grove, PhD, who sparked my interest in the application of transformational change in the United States. My passion for the development and implementation of strategy and major change initiatives was fueled by her relentless discussions of sponsorship and corporate culture in US-based organizations. I am grateful that Karen introduced me to corporate America and the world of consulting in the United States.

In writing this book, I have appreciated the helpful comments and endless revisions of each chapter by my friend Marita Klein, PhD. Marita is a native South African and industrial psychologist. Her professional knowledge and language skills were invaluable in completing this project.

I am thankful for my colleagues in South Africa. Together we spent years dealing with people on both sides of the political spectrum, introducing new ideas and dealing with their reactions that pushed the country to the edge of civil war and destruction. Those experiences shaped my thoughts and understanding of human nature and change. I salute those who paid the ultimate sacrifice.

My wife, Janettha, is the spark behind this work. She was persistent in telling me that I should capture the main elements in book format. She believed in me and provided endless support. Thank you.

# Introduction

A physical therapist once told me she worked for two different organizations over the past five years: a local hospital and an elementary school district. Her job descriptions at both locations were similar and focused on her professional services. There was no reference to the hospital's or school district's strategy or related goals. I asked if she had any knowledge of the main organizational strategy of either organization. She could only point to a poster on the wall with some strategy-related information on it. Since my conversation with her, I have approached several CEOs, and they shared similar experiences. One CEO walked through the building and asked random employees if they knew what the company's strategy was. Responses varied from "I have no clue" to a brief reference to some presentation or poster. When asked how they personally contribute to the strategy, their responses were even more telling. They related that by doing their perspective jobs "as good as I can," they will help promote the strategy. The CEO also inquired whether there was any mention of the strategy in their job descriptions. The overwhelming response was "no."

I suggested that the CEOs also ask employees to explain how the strategy he introduced at the beginning of the year impacted their performance. The stunning finding was that except for the 1 percent of the employees who are executives in the organizations, there was no link between employees' performance and the strategy.

What will happen if you ask similar questions in your organization? What do you anticipate the responses will be? Will you be surprised to learn that the strategy—which is critical to you as the CEO, board member, or executive—is fundamentally disconnected from the rest of the organization? Michael LeBoeuf wrote, "You get what you reward." If the strategy is not a reality in people's minds and not reflected in their job descriptions and performance reviews, it is no wonder the strategies point in one direction while the organization maintains the direction perpetuated in the workers' job descriptions and performance reviews. There is a disparity here. No wonder the vast majority of new strategies failed to deliver the intended results.

For the past several years I explored the reasons strategies fail outright in delivering their intended results. I concluded that in many organizations, the strategy is not connected to the individuals in those organizations. Employees have to know what their organization's strategy is and how their day-to-day activities support it. This connection can only be developed and implemented in a change-enabling milieu. There must be an organizational environment that embraces change through meaningful engagement of those impacted by the strategy. Organizations have a responsibility to those employees who are accountable for supporting the strategy through their actions. Organizations should anchor strategies in the workers' job descriptions and performance reviews. These connections, when developed and maintained will significantly increase the odds that the strategy will deliver the intended results.

Organizations can no longer afford to squander valuable resources due to their inability to successfully develop and implement a strategy. I will address these issues in detail. A brief discussion related to organizational strategy is followed by an in-depth discussion about how to adjust a current organizational setting into a change-enabling one. The remainder of the book discusses the three critical connections that drives the adoption of an organizational strategy: the psychological, structural, and contractual connections.

## CHAPTER ONE

# Strategy x Adoption = Results

## Strategy

Organizations develop and implement strategies to solve a specific business problem. The problem can be one of many (e.g., losing market share, decreased revenue, or decreased profitability). Once a problem is identified, stakeholders fixate on the numbers—the business results. They ask fundamental questions, such as, "What is happening in the market?" "How are our competitors doing?" and "How can we stay ahead of the pack?" If the current results are not satisfactory, stakeholders start to think about ways for the organization to be more successful—to obtain better results. The dissatisfaction with the current state or the desire for a vision of a better future creates the impetus for change. Energy is unleashed, strategic momentum is built, and the organization starts to explore new ways of becoming successful.

Organizations design and implement strategies to take advantage of opportunities. An agile organization has the ability to identify and decisively seize opportunities in the market. Organizations may want to aggressively enter new markets, rapidly establish and scale up a new business, and perhaps bet heavily on new technology. This becomes the strategic intent of the organization—the ambitious and compelling dream that energizes the organization in pursuing success. The strategic intent provides the emotional and motivational fuel for the journey to the future. Strategies are designed, developed, and implemented to realize these dreams. It all comes down to business results—the current results and the desire for improved results.

In today's highly competitive environment, companies that become complacent are the losers. Global competition, technology, and fewer barriers to entering the market force organizations to constantly evolve, deploy new functionalities, acquire new capabilities, or migrate existing capabilities and compete in new markets, to name but a few demands. These potential changes have to translate into business strategies to make them executable—to make them real and able to achieve the desired results.

In slower times, organizations could develop their strategies, create barriers for others to enter their markets, and implement and allow their strategies to unfold and realize over time. For many companies, this is no longer feasible. Organizations and strategies have to yield results faster than ever before. The speed factor significantly raises the bar for strategy development and implementation. Now more than ever, organizations have to select the right strategy, develop it fully, implement it effectively, and obtain results expediently.

A change in strategy represents a change in direction or focus, and subsequently a change in behavior. In very small companies, this does not present a big problem—everybody knows what they are trying to accomplish and what they have to do to make it happen. As organizations grow and layers of complexity are added, it becomes harder to execute a change. In mature organizations with a high level of institutionalization, change becomes even more cumbersome. The challenge is to be as nimble and agile as a small organization while taking advantage of the organization's mature capabilities. Strategies are only successful if they yield results. Despite huge organizational investment in strategy management, only approximately 37 percent of strategies realize their intended results. The other 63 percent vary from partial success to outright failure (Mankins & Steele, *HBR*, January 2006). I have looked at strategies that did not yield the intended results and next describe the range of outcomes.

Some organizations develop and implement a new strategy. However, the strategy does not yield the expected results, although the strategy implementation went smoothly and the execution was done well. For example, an organization planned to increase revenue by $400M through mergers and acquisitions (M&A) but fell short on the delivery. This happens frequently due to a wide array of circumstances. In this situation, the combined revenue potential was overestimated and overlapping markets were not visible during the due diligence phase of the merger.

Organizations develop and implement a new strategy but fail to implement it fully. For example, a large health-care system on the West Coast suspended the implementation of electronic clinical medical records after completing a quarter of all their hospitals. This may happen when the designed strategy only gains partial traction, which may result in partial implementation. Partial implementations happen frequently, are costly, and never deliver the expected results.

A strategy can fade away when an organization develops and launches this new strategy with big fanfare but lets it "hang out to dry" over time. It often happens that once the strategy has been launched, it faces several challenges. Maintaining momentum, producing the expected results, and sustaining support by the leadership are just a few of the challenges. Rather than addressing these challenges, the leaders of the organization simply stop talking about it. They turn their attention to day-to-day operations and choke the strategy to death with their silence. This fading is visible when sponsorship for the strategy is tracked over time. Support for the strategy never gains traction at the lower levels and loses sponsorship at the top. When this happens, the new strategy just slowly fades away.

Some strategies are outright abandoned before realization. A strategy to increase revenue through an M&A failed due to a lack of trust. An M&A between a national accounting firm and a smaller regional accounting firm was stopped just before the final stage when new information related to liabilities surfaced. The national accounting firm was going to assume the liabilities of the smaller regional firm during the M&A. A lack of transparency with regard to the critical liabilities created a significant lack of trust, killing the M&A and the strategy to increase their revenue.

In another situation, a large regional health-care provider launched a strategy to centralize their accounting/billing functions. They abandoned the strategy midway when it became apparent that the individual hospitals would have to give up control over their billing functions, and they were not ready to agree to that. Their refusal brought the implementation to a halt, and the organization abandoned the strategy. Consequently, the large regional health-care provider lost hundreds of millions of dollars due to unused systems and associated development costs.

Often strategies are changed before the original design delivers any results. Walmart implemented a new strategy to reduce product variety during a sluggish economy. After the strategy was implemented, it became clear that their customers did not like the changes. The retailer adapted the strategy by increasing variety again, albeit not to previous levels.

Clearly the level of success of strategy implementation can range from full realization to outright failure. Fundamentally, the results of a strategy are a reflection of the milieu in which the implementation took place, leaving a history in its path that will also impact future implementations.

Successful strategy implementations have the following potential positive consequences: Analysts on Wall Street, shareholders, and/or partners celebrate when a new strategy delivers the intended results. A successful strategy elevates the organization in the marketplace. The organization encourages its achievements and will attract new clients and investors. In addition, it will attract high-quality talent. An organization that can develop and implement a strategy delivering results instills trust in stakeholders that will facilitate future initiatives.

A successful implementation demonstrates the leadership's ability to assess the marketplace, design a good quality strategy, implement it, and sustain the changes long enough to yield the intended results. A successful implementation leaves behind outdated structures and approaches and utilizes practices that can be leveraged in any future changes. Successful strategy implementations make the organization more agile and able to implement changes more effectively.

In contrast, failed strategy implementation may have the following negative consequences. A failed strategy creates a legacy of failure and erodes trust. It creates a ripple effect throughout the organization and client base. The failure may become part of the company's organizational history and make future changes harder to implement. In addition, a failed strategy undermines trust in the organization, and, more specifically, weakens trust in the leadership. These ripple effects will hamper the organization in executing normal day-to-day operations as well as future implementations.

A weakening of trust and a legacy of failure will not only hamper the introduction of a new strategy, its impact becomes more visible in the form of sluggishness. Individuals, reluctant to change because of previous failures, want more proof and engage in more detailed conversations that might slow down the change process, resulting in sluggishness. A failed strategy can cause an organization to lose traction in the market. The organization starts to fall behind competitors, especially those competitors that are successful in implementing new strategies.

Failed strategy implementations have a direct effect on investor confidence and contributions. There are plenty of examples of investors withdrawing their investments when it became clear that a strategy was not going to yield the intended results. In the face of a strategy implementation failure, business analysts may downgrade the investment potential, resulting in a withdrawal of investments or hesitation to invest. This may lead to a downward spiral of an organization's stock value.

Organizations with a legacy of failed strategy implementations are also hindered in their attempts to attract top talent, and existing talent may even leave the organization. This may lead to an overall reduction in competitiveness due to decreased internal talent. Strategy implementation failures are costly. In addition to the financial costs, there are costs in terms of resources allocation and time spent, which could have been used otherwise.

Strategy failure can result in a personal cost to leaders as it affects their reputation and impedes upward mobility. This situation can only be rectified when they can demonstrate their ability to successfully implement a strategy.

Strategies can realize their intended results if organizations focus on the fact that the results of a strategy are the product of the quality of the strategy and the adoption thereof.

## Strategy x Adoption = Results

It is not only important to design and develop a meaningful, valid strategy, organizations should invest equally in the adoption of the strategy in order for it to yield the intended results. A relatively weak strategy, fully adopted, has the inherent potential to yield better results than a brilliant strategy that is not well adopted.

The success of a strategy thus hinges on the selection of a valid strategy as well as its adoption. Most organizations spend a significant amount of resources on strategy selection, and although there are examples of "wrong" strategies, they are few and far between and are not the focus of this book. More often, strategies do not yield the intended results because the behavior changes that the new strategy requires were not adopted to the extent that it could start to yield the intended results. The behavior changes were not adopted because organizations struggled to effectively implement the strategy. This begets the question of how organizations can implement a strategy more effectively and efficiently to create the environment in which the strategy will yield the intended results.

As professionals, we were interested in understanding why this is happening. We researched failed strategy implementations and started to pay attention to what was happening while working in organizations. My observations did not reveal a single source of failure but a conglomeration of events that occur regularly in many organizations. For example, the strategy was developed without engaging everybody; the strategy was delegated from operational leaders to staff for implementation; the strategy was never articulated into specific behaviors at all levels; and the strategy did not impose consequences for people who did not change their behavior to be aligned with the strategy. These events all fall within the domain of "strategy implementation and adoption," not "strategy selection and development."

As research and observations indicate, any one of these adoption issues will not necessarily condemn a strategy implementation—if enough of these events happen in an organization, the strategy will not live in the behaviors of its members or the organization and will fail. We call this "connection." Connection is the link between the strategy and the individuals in an organization and is the foundation of strategy adoption. The stronger this connection, the higher the level of adoption of the strategy, which ultimately enables it to yield the intended results. The gateway to adoption is through developing and ensuring connection within a change-enabling milieu and maintaining the connection until the strategy is yielding the intended results. Strategic failure occurs when the organization does not have the ability to make the connection, or when the connection has not been established. The connection will be weak and brittle and break under minimum strain or when the connection cannot be maintained through the life cycle of the strategy (it breaks before the strategy can realize the intent).

Organizations can create and maintain this connection through an integrated holistic approach of strategy development and implementation that connects and maintains a connection throughout the strategy life cycle. The connection consists of three different subconnections:

- a psychological connection to the individual (the organization's response to human need for information and structure during change)

- a structural connection to the whole organization (the business-planning process), and

- a contractual connection to the individual (job description, performance review, and incentives).

This integrated approach is deployed throughout the organization through sponsorship in a change-enabling milieu.

The first challenge is to connect the strategy *psychologically* to all the individuals in the organization. Fundamentally, the psychological connection unlocks individuals' willingness to abandon current misaligned behavior and adopt the newly required strategy-aligned behavior. An organization has to persuade individuals that they need to change their day-to-day activities and will help them through this process. We call this process the psychological connection, and it concerns the organization's response to individuals' need for information and structure during change.

If organizations fail at making the psychological connection, it becomes evident, such as in the following issue, where there is little or no trust in the solution. For example, in a national accounting firm, the new strategy called for the outsourcing of individual tax services. Partners in the firm and staff indicated a strong opposition to the idea. They didn't think outsourcing would solve the business problem or meet the needs of their clients, and they did not trust a third party with their clients' data. This kind of verbal resistance is always a clear indication that the strategy and the local leaders are not connected, and unless addressed, the strategy cannot be successful.

During the implementation of electronic clinical medical records at a local Phoenix hospital, some physicians clearly stated that they didn't see why they should enter any data into the electronic file of the patient since a paper chart is much easier to maintain and readily available. The physicians did not trust the solution, and therefore could not connect the strategy to themselves at a personal or individual level.

Both observations point to a disconnect between the new strategy and those who had to change their behavior for the strategy to succeed. They did not trust the solution and could not see themselves changing their behavior in the way the strategy demanded. The psychological connection was not established. If all impacted people are unwilling to adapt their behavior in accordance with the strategy, no sustainable changes will take place and the strategy is doomed. There is a strong relationship between the quality of the psychological connection and the individual's willingness to change and adopt the new strategy.

If an organization engages in creating the psychological connection, it acknowledges that individuals need to go on a journey from unawareness of the new strategy to adoption of it. In order to complete this journey successfully, they need specific sequential information and structure. It is the organization's responsibility to provide such information and structure in order to succeed. Most organizations have a change-management process that they follow, and although it sometimes brings about some change, it seldom creates significant or lasting individual change. This happens when the organization's response to the human need for information and structure is not adequately addressed during the implementation. The individual never connects with the strategy and thus does not change the necessary beliefs and day-to-day actions to make the strategy successful.

The second challenge is to connect the strategy *structurally* to the organization. Fundamentally, the structural connection identifies the specific behaviors an individual needs to change to align with the new strategy. This is done through the business-planning process. If organizations fail in the structural connection, it soon becomes evident. In reviewing the business plans of AAV Pharmaceuticals local offices, it became apparent that the people who developed the business plans and those who developed the strategy were not communicating. There was little evidence of the link between the business plan and the strategy's goals and drivers. Surprisingly, there was very little change even in the business plans following the implementation.

For example, an organization intended to increase its market share from 14.6 percent to 20 percent over three years. However, when we added all the cascaded market share growth targets at the local level, it only came to 17.9 percent nationally. There was no reconciliation between the targets set at local levels and the main goals of the strategy. Both observations point to a disconnect between the strategy and the core functions in the organization. It is clear that the quality of the structural connection significantly increases the odds of a successful strategy implementation.

To create the structural connection, the organization needs to translate the strategy into four to six strategic drivers that, if executed upon, will realize the intended result. These drivers are translated into action steps, integrated into the business-planning process, and subsequently cascaded down to the lowest level of the organization, enabling every individual to know which strategically aligned actions are needed at his or her level to yield the intended results.

The third key challenge is a *contractual* connection from the strategy to every individual in the organization. Why does the strategy need to be connected in this way? The contractual connection fundamentally anchors the required aligned behaviors in the job description and performance review of the individual, thereby restructuring the contractual arrangement between the individual and the organization. This is paramount in driving accountability and the sustainability of the strategy. Individuals tend to do what is specified in their job descriptions and especially the actions that are reflected in their performance reviews; their rewards or incentives are tied to it.

In mature organizations, the job descriptions are usually done by professional class (e.g., accountant, psychologist, business development) and reflect the general role of the job, rather than the specific strategic actions needed in a specific organization. Individuals identify themselves as part of a role (e.g., "I am in sales," or "I am a manager in the distribution department"). These role descriptions become part of the individual's identity. If a strategy is not directly reflected in the individual job description, it hovers in limbo and becomes "something they want us to do" but does not carry weight and impact with the individual. The individual does not feel personally responsible for realizing the actions the strategy calls for but only feels responsible for performing the actions their generic job description calls for. It is therefore imperative that the strategy gets anchored through the contractual connection. Elements of the strategy, applicable to the individual, should be written into his/her individual job description. As the strategy becomes part of a person's job description, it is anchored at the individual level.

In the same vein, if the individual performance review is not changed to reflect the strategy, individuals will revert back to the behavior they are measured by. The same goes for the reward system. We have often observed that managers get the maximum bonus, although their departments missed their strategic revenue goals. This practice is defended on the basis of fairness. Once again, the organization failed to create a connection between the strategy and the individual—in this case, an individual who determines what subordinates do. A strategy can never succeed if all individuals do not feel responsible for making it happen and if the organization does not anchor it contractually.

Organizations' failure to create the contractual connections is easily identified, as the strategy is not reflected in job descriptions, performance reviews, and the rewards systems. In reviewing a sample of job descriptions in organizations, it was discovered that individuals' job descriptions were similar to what is found in the majority of organizations. The position of manager is defined in terms of the role. The job description is 90 percent generic, with very few specifics. And there is no link in the job description to the organization's strategy. Why is this important? We know that a job description is the foundation for people's annual assessment. Since the performance appraisal is based on the job description and not linked to the strategy, the strategy is therefore not connected to the individual. He or she will execute according to the job description regardless of what needs to be done to get the organization to move in the direction of the strategy.

The performance review of an individual in the IT department was also reviewed. Her job description was essentially generic—similar to all IT staff. The performance review assessed her performance against her job description. Once again, it was noted that her performance assessment was not connected to her organization's strategy. When the new strategy was implemented, no changes were made to her job description. This broken link reinforced the fact that the organization's strategy called for a change in one direction. By not changing her performance appraisal to something more negative to reflect her ignoring or refusing to adhere to the organization's strategy, she was basically "rewarded" for not changing. Unless this changes as well, the strategy will never get the traction it needs to succeed.

The rewards allocation of a director was also reviewed. She received the maximum bonus despite her department missing its revenue goals. There was no connection between the allocation of her bonus and the results the strategy called for. This situation was aggravated by the fact that all the directors received similar bonuses under the fairness policy. When a strategy is not linked to rewards, nobody is compelled to change his or her behavior in support of the strategy.

These examples point to a failure to establish a contractual connection during the strategy implementation. As long as job descriptions, performance reviews, and rewards and recognition do not reflect the new strategy, people will continue to execute on the implicit contract established in the job description. Almost all the organizations that reported a failed strategy did not anchor their new strategy at the individual level.

The psychological, structural, and contractual connections collectively drive the strategy's level of adoption. If an organization succeeds in establishing and maintaining these connections, the strategy will be acted upon and the intended results can be realized.

Implementing the strategy and making these connections do not occur in a vacuum. The connections have to be made within a distinctive organizational environment with characteristics that can either help or hinder the adoption.

Here's an analogy. Building a new road across a swamp, the environment necessitates us to address the environmental conditions before road construction can start. The characteristics of the swamp have the potential to grind any building project to a halt. Similarly, the inherent characteristics of an organization often pose significant challenges to the implementation of any strategy. The organization's history, culture, level of trust, sponsorship, and expectations are all part of this distinct environment. These elements need to be assessed and adapted in order to become a change-enabling milieu. We will pay significant attention to the organizational situation to enable us to develop a solid strategy implementation process. The process will significantly increase the adoption of the new strategy.

The quality of the connections within a change-enabling milieu will significantly increase the level of adoption, resulting in the successful implementation of the strategy. The results of a strategy are the product of the quality of the strategy and the level of adoption. A broader understanding of the results of strategy implementations will enhance our ability to develop high quality connections, elevating the level of adoption.

The quality of the adoption pivots on the strength of the connections and the change-enabling milieu. This begets the question of what the consequences of the absence of a connection or a weak connection are. Executives' inability to establish the identified psychological, structural, or contractual connections leads to failure. If the connections are not made, there will be little adoption of the behavior necessary to realize the strategy. Organizations make large investments during the development and implementation of new strategies. However, they often fail to connect the strategy to all impacted individuals. It is this connection between the strategy and individuals that is needed to translate the ideas, in the mind of the leaders, into concepts on paper and actions for the individual. Without these connections, any new strategy is at high risk of failure due to a low level of adoption.

In most organizations, the connections are often unintentionally developed rather than deliberately architected or designed, resulting in weak, brittle connections. The connections are weak, and the slightest pressure results in a disconnect between the strategy and the impacted individuals. Weak connections are especially dangerous. They create the impression that all is well and put the executives at ease. However, a connection can quickly fail, resulting in the derailment of the strategy before the executives can repair the connection.

Sometimes there are connections that have been deliberately developed but were severed by the impacted individuals. The development of the necessary connections does not guarantee they will last as long as needed. Connections should be monitored in order to detect a disconnect and subsequently activate a contingency plan to repair the disconnect. Once a connection has disconnected, it will not repair itself and will stay disconnected until the strategy fails and the connection is no longer needed or executives intervene and repair it.

## Summary

A strategy is evaluated by the results it yields. Organizations spend considerable time and resources selecting and developing new strategies to solve business problems or address market needs. Despite this investment, many strategies fail to realize their intent. We argue that the success of a strategy is the product of the quality of the strategy and the level of adoption. Organizations often pay more attention to the development of the strategy and very little attention to its adoption. The consequence is often a high level of failure. Organizations must elevate their focus on strategy adoption.

The level of adoption of a strategy is dependent on an organization's ability to create connections between the strategy and all impacted individuals. The first task should be to create a change-enabling milieu. Secondly, they have to make the connections that are the psychological connections that unlock individuals' willingness to change behavior, the structural connection that flashes out the details around those changes, and the contractual connection that anchors the strategy to the individual. If an organization succeeds in making the connections, the chances of a successful strategy implementation significantly increase.

In this book, the focus will not be on the selection and development of a strategy. The focus will be on implementation and adoption of strategies. Upcoming chapters will discuss in detail how organizations can create and maintain these connections through an integrated, holistic approach to strategy development and implementation that connects and maintains the connections throughout the strategy's life cycle. This integrated approach is deployed throughout the organization through sponsorship in a change-enabling milieu. A solid understanding of adoption and its subcomponents will enable executives to embrace the idea, bringing balance to the strategy implementation while significantly increasing the potential for success.

## CHAPTER TWO
# Change-Enabling Milieu

Over time, organizations, like people, seem to have a certain "personality." They tend to develop a characteristic way of doing and being. This "personality" is evident in their culture, trust, history, expectations, communication, and sponsorship. All strategy implementations and change endeavors that take place within this specific environment can either be change enhancing or change inhibiting. Knowing and understanding the organizational milieu is one of the first tasks to accomplish in strategy development and implementation. The second task is to enhance the milieu in such a way that it facilitates and sustains the implementation.

The development of the three connections between the strategy and the impacted individuals can be done more effectively and efficiently within a change-enabling milieu. This chapter highlights the characteristics of the organizational needs that must be assessed, with specific focus on the critical elements of sponsorship and communication.

## Culture

According to J. E. Kralewski, et al., in their article "Culture as a Management Tool for Medical Groups" (*Physician Exec*, 2008 Sep–Oct; 34(5):12–4, 16–8), organizational culture is "a social or normative glue that holds together a potentially diverse group of organizational members." An organization's culture is similar to an individual's personality.

Edgar H. Schein defines "culture" as, "A pattern of shared basic assumptions that the group learned as it solved its problems of external adaptation and internal integration that has worked well enough to be considered valid and, therefore, to be taught [to new members] as the correct way you perceive, think, and feel in relation to those problems" (http://www.tnellen.com/ted/tc/schein.html).

Culture as such is a broad, encompassing subject. Shared beliefs are the main cultural elements that are relevant in strategy implementation and will be our main focus.

Culture is observed in individual and group behavior and by what people say. It is critical to recognize that all observable aspects of culture are linked to certain beliefs and assumptions. Therefore, all actions are—intentionally or unintentionally, strongly or loosely—linked to beliefs. Through shared beliefs, behavioral norms are determined and followed in organizations. Fundamentally, beliefs drive behavior.

A new strategy calls for a change in some behaviors in the day-to-day activities of all employees. They are expected to discontinue some of their present behaviors or actions and adopt new behaviors or actions. Without the change in behavior, things will continue the current way and a new strategy will not be adopted. It is thus imperative to recognize the role of beliefs in the successful implementation of strategy. The underlying beliefs that drive the current behavior have to be made visible and need to be addressed before any behavior change can take place. The traditional models of strategy development and implementation do not fully address the impact that beliefs have on organizational culture. This is a serious oversight which increases the odds that, at some point, the strategy implementation will be in opposition to some underlying, unacknowledged beliefs that drive the behavior of many. If the new strategy is in opposition to some strongly held beliefs, individuals will stay connected to those beliefs and will not be able to connect psychologically to the new strategy, resulting in an unsuccessful strategy implementation.

The following questions are crucial in strategy implementation:

- What main beliefs that underscore the organization's current strategy have been uncovered?

- Are these beliefs in alignment with the new strategy?

If you can provide a clear answer to these questions, you are addressing the core issues of the new strategy. If not, the new strategy implementation is at risk.

To change behaviors, the beliefs that drive the behavior have to be identified. If the specific belief is altered, then an opportunity to change the behavior is created. If the belief is permanently altered, then the behavior changes become more sustainable.

Individuals have hundreds of beliefs that drive their behavior; cumulatively, an organization may not be able to understand all the underlying operant beliefs, especially since bigger organizations often have a complex culture. The challenge is not to try to understand all aspects of organizational culture but to identify those few critical beliefs that underscore the new strategy and to recognize any diametrically opposed beliefs.

The identification of beliefs is not only challenging but outright difficult. It is this embedded difficulty that deters most executives from fully addressing this issue and subsequently failing to reach or exceed their strategic goals. Uncovering the beliefs takes an in-depth understanding of culture, as well as the skill to uncover the beliefs through behavior interpretation. Once the potential beliefs have been uncovered, they need to be validated by sharing the findings. This process allows everybody to recognize the underlying beliefs.

Let's take an example from the accounting industry to demonstrate the issue. In this company, the CEO, John Vought,[1] wants to deploy a strategy where one of the critical drivers is marketing and sales by accounting professionals. The cultural assessment identifies an opposing belief, namely "accounting professionals are responsible for interpreting accounting laws, assessing adherence to the laws, and providing professional opinions to this effect." This belief drives specific behaviors, such as a great reluctance by the professionals to personally participate in marketing and sales, and they would rather appoint business-development experts to do the marketing and sales for them.

The accounting professionals' belief developed over a long time, starting with their education, where the curriculum for CPAs included little or no material related to marketing and sales of their own services. During their early careers, business-development executives in the firm did the marketing and sales, thus further reinforcing this belief. The final step in solidifying this belief was reinforced when they earned their bonuses without having gotten involved with marketing and sales. The CEO believed differently and wanted them responsible and accountable for their own marketing and sales, although this strategy would be inconsistent with current practices and underlying

---

1     John Vought is a fictitious name.

beliefs. The implementation of this section of the new strategy still struggles to get traction and has not moved forward.

Development of beliefs takes a long time and is strengthened by systemic encouragement and reinforced by organizations. Dismantling old beliefs to the point where new behavior can be sustained takes focus and effort.

Culture can enable the organization to create the three critical connections in which case culture will not be a significant factor during the implementation of the strategy. This, however, is a rare occurrence. In most cases, some shared cultural beliefs may prevent the strategy from getting connected right out of the gate or may disconnect the strategy when those impacted discover the inconsistency between their current beliefs and the beliefs the strategy call for. Until the beliefs are uncovered, the new strategy will seemingly be accepted at a high level, sending a potential "false" signal to the executives that the strategy has been accepted.

During one of the steps of the implementation, those impacted need to determine how the strategy will affect them personally. It is during this discovery phase that the impacted employees will realize one of the intended outcomes of the new strategy is that they have to get out of their offices, meet with their current and prospective clients, and engage in typical marketing and sales activities. The expectations are inconsistent with their beliefs and they disconnect from the strategy. They will stay disconnected until the underlying belief is addressed.

Once individuals disconnect from the strategy, the implementation is at risk because strategy-aligned behavior is not adopted. What makes the situation even more complicated is that people are impacted differently, resulting in disconnects at different times. Executives start to receive mixed messages; some that the strategy is great and needed, others indicating the strategy will not work and that it is going in the wrong direction. This is a direct result of individuals discovering the conflicting beliefs during the implementation. Executives tend to focus on the positive messages and do not always recognize that a disconnect is about to take place, hidden in the negative messages. This confusion puts the strategy implementation at risk because the executives are blindsided by the disconnect and do not develop timely mitigation.

In order to create a change-enabling milieu, the underlying cultural beliefs need to be taken into consideration and navigated to such an extent that the connections can be established, and disconnections must proactively be prevented. Should a disconnect still take place as a result of culture, it needs to be detected and reconnected.

## Culture in a Change-Enabling Milieu

How do we navigate the complexity of culture and change elements of the culture in such a way that it becomes a change-enabling milieu?

Let's look at the navigating strategy by means of an analogy. Imagine being in a sailboat on a lake, wanting to sail from the western to the eastern shore. With luck, a westerly wind is blowing. This presents an ideal environment where you have to get the wind behind your sails to travel to the eastern shore. Upon reaching the eastern shore, you realize that the wind is still coming strongly out of the west, but now you wish to return. This poses a more challenging environment where you can't sail directly west but can reach your goal through tacking your way back, which requires significantly more time and effort.

Culture has similar characteristics. If a new strategy is built upon the same basic beliefs as the current strategy, the organization will have a smooth implementation from a cultural perspective. However, if the new strategy is inconsistent with the current culture and beliefs, then the goal could be reached through tacking, which implies more time and resources. A problem that often occurs is that an organization sets out from one shoreline to the other with a fixed schedule indicating when to reach the destination. It starts sailing with no wind, only to get trapped in the middle of the journey when strong headwinds threaten to derail the journey. How can we prevent this from happening?

**Be proactive:** Conduct a current and desired assessment interactively in order to discover the beliefs that may be in the way while at the same time constructing the new strategy. This will help navigate around some of the cultural issues and only confront the one or two cultural issues that are non-negotiable. Develop specific plans to mitigate the identified risk in advance, and this will result in proactive mitigation.

**Identify the disconnect:** The disconnect can be observed in resistance-related behavior of those impacted. They might make comments such as, "I am not a sales person, I am an accountant," "The strategy will not work," "I am not trained to do marketing and sales," "What is marketing doing?"

"I don't have time for this." Resistance is natural and normal, and if the resistance-related behavior can be identified, it should be viewed as a gift, because if the leadership pays attention to it and connects the dots, they can learn which problems need to be mitigated. It all points to the employees' belief systems about their roles as accounting professionals and the fact that they are not comfortable with their own marketing and sales competency.

**Reconnect a broken link:** If a broken link is discovered through resistance-related behavior, it needs to be mitigated by addressing the resistance issues rather than a direct attack of the beliefs. To alter beliefs that developed over time is counterproductive and a resource nightmare. Without oversimplifying resistance, we can describe the fuel of resistance in terms of a lack of willingness or a lack of ability. People will often hide their lack of ability or confidence in their ability behind unwillingness, resulting in the "wrong" mitigation. For example, it is easier to say "the strategy won't work" than to admit they don't have the skills to be successful in the new strategy. The most productive focal point, with the best sustainable results, is ability. People resist change because they believe they don't have the skills or abilities to adopt the new behavior. Going back to the example, the accountants will not do marketing and sales at the level the new strategy calls for because they believe it is not their job and that they don't have the skills to be successful at it. Knowing this, you need to use the principle of tack. In a strategy when you cannot directly obtain results, you have to leverage and navigate the internal characteristics of the organization (e.g., culture, consuming additional time and resources). In this example, they had to commit time and resources to provide partners with the opportunity to become competent in marketing and sales. As you complete the competency development, you can reconnect the strategy to the partners by leveraging rewards and recognition. This will keep the employees engaged as long as needed to systematically change their belief system, creating sustainable change.

**Beliefs drive behaviors:** Culture is visible through behaviors and what people say. Strategy calls for a change in behaviors, subsequently a change in beliefs. It is important to ensure that beliefs are aligned with the behavior the new strategy calls for to create a change-enabling milieu. Once identified, determine the effort it will take to neutralize the belief's effect on the strategy. It is of utmost importance to keep culture on the radar at all times due to its subtlety. It is difficult to see it for what it is, and we normally underestimate its impact on change.

# Trust in a Change-Enabling Milieu

Trust is fundamental to a healthy and dynamic organization. Not all organizations enjoy the same level of trust. Trust also fluctuates within organizations over time. A critical question is, "Will the current level of trust enhance the development and implementation of a new strategy, or will it erode the foundations of the strategy to the point of failure?"

Trust is a relational construct that pivots on perceptions of competency and intent. Competency and intent are both crucial during a strategy implementation. Do the stakeholders in the organization believe that the leader of the organization has everybody's best interest at heart? If the leader's intent is trusted, do the employees trust that the leader and the rest of the organization have the required competence to succeed? Many organizations have a history of strategy implementations that did not deliver the expected results. How can an organization overcome its history and create the trust necessary to have a successful implementation? How can trust become part of the change-enabling milieu?

Different elements of trust need to be developed during a strategy implementation. The first is trust in the leader. This is developed through the leader's actions, leadership, and words during the implementation. Individuals also need to trust the solution. This is done through engaging, collaborating, and designing an implementation that creates an environment where people can think about the solution, change their behavior to be aligned to it, and see the results of the solution. In effect, the leader now returns the favor of trust by allowing people to develop trust in the solution.

People also need to develop trust in themselves. They need to see themselves as successful and competent in the new strategy before they will commit to it wholeheartedly. The organization can help them develop trust in their ability by supporting them through effective sponsorship, while they experiment with new behaviors, develop new skills and competencies, and learn to adjust. The trust is cemented when the individual knows this is a lasting change in which he or she can be successful and that the organization also views it as such by changing the job description and performance review to reflect the changes.

The final element that needs to be developed is that of trusting others in the organization. A strategy implementation affects many individuals, and

21

they want evidence that others are also making the necessary corrections. As lessons learned are shared, mutual trust is developed.

The organization has a responsibility to create a change-enabling milieu in which these levels of trust can be developed. This should contain solid, trustworthy leadership, transparency, engagement, and collaboration. The cycle of trust bestowed, earned, and extended can significantly increase the success of any strategy implementation and create a lasting effect on corporate culture, allowing future efforts to be faster, cheaper, and more effective.

## Trust—a Rudimentary Asset

According to Dr. Duane C. Tway Jr. in his 1993 dissertation "A Construct of Trust," trust is "the state of readiness for unguarded interaction with someone or something." He calls trust a construct because it is "constructed" of three components: "the capacity for trusting, the perception of competence, and the perception of intentions."

The perceptions of competence and intentions are especially important in strategy implementation. The capacity for trust is developed over a long time based on history and experience. Changing an individual's capacity for trust in the short run is not that easily accomplished.

What, then, is the link between the perceptions of competency, intentions, and strategy implementation?

Trust is a rudimentary asset for any senior executive. When executives develop a new strategy, they seek and expect improved results. In addition, a new strategy calls for new behaviors by those impacted. However, those impacted individuals are highly unlikely to change their current behavior if they don't trust their executive leadership. Their trust, or lack thereof, is fueled by two perceptions: competence and intentions.

It is of utmost importance to executive leadership that there is enough trust when a new strategy is introduced. Without it, a CEO will have trouble selling the strategy to the board, senior executives, and employees. If there is insufficient trust, the probability that individuals will adopt sustainable behavioral changes is slim to none. The key questions are, "How do you create sustainable trust in an organization?" And even more, "How do you create trust to the level where it will excel the implementation of the strategy and reduce time and cost?"

The need to develop and implement a new strategy creates a significant opportunity in an organization, if done correctly, to increase the general level of trust in the organization, which can help further organizational endeavors. Stephen M. R. Covey's research on trust in the workplace concludes that trust lowers costs and increases the speed of change (Covey, 2006). The implementation process can serve as a trust-building vehicle in an organization that will benefit the executive leadership as well as the organization itself. Our focus is to enable trust to become a central element in the change-enabling milieu.

How does the organization, using the strategy-implementation process, enable stakeholders to develop the comprehensive trust that will accelerate the process and drive the associated costs down?

## Trust in the Leader

Tway concluded that the perception of competence and intentions are key elements in trust building (Tway, 1993). The perceptions of those impacted by the strategy are greatly influenced by the behavior of the leader. The actions of the leader can be described in terms of creating a change-enabling milieu and by leading the change by example and with his or her words. Those impacted by the strategy-related changes develop trust in their leader as they experience his or her competent actions.

Let's look at those actions that have the greatest impact on the perception of competency.

**Developing sponsors:** Those impacted by the strategy need specific information, structure, and support from their sponsor in order for them to discover where and how they must change their behavior to align with the new strategy. They have probably experienced different levels and quality sponsorship in the past and know that not all of management will sponsor the strategy well. Trust is built when they notice that the entire management team has received sponsorship training and they experience efficient sponsorship service.

**Merging key processes:** All employees have experienced calls for change, often in a haphazard way, which did not really lead to significant, sustained change. When they experience well-thought-out and well-coordinated efforts, with significant opportunities to participate at their level during the implementation, it builds more trust. Being part of the solution conveys to them that they are valued and increases their collaboration and trust. Key processes to be merged are strategy development, business development, and the individual change process.

**Providing a roadmap:** Trust is increased when the leader produces a clearly-defined end-to-end strategy-implementation roadmap. Even if individuals do not agree with the map, they are trusted with the process and given the opportunity to define their role in the implementation. There is a significant trust-building opportunity if you clearly define what you are going to do and then execute it.

**Focusing on the individual:** Individuals need specific sequential information and support during the change process in order to unlock their willingness to adopt behaviors that will make them successful in the new strategy. There is a corporate responsibility to provide this information and structure, which is often overlooked. By creating a strategy implementation that really takes individuals' needs into account, the stress on the individual is lessened as he or she feels heard and taken care of during the process. This plays a significant part in forging the psychological connection and building trust.

**Cascading:** Those impacted by the strategy want to make a positive contribution to the success of the organization. Trust is built when the individual knows, for example, that the intent of the strategy is to increase organizational revenue by $500m over the next four years and can clearly see how his personal contribution of $50k will help realize the overarching goal. Through cascading of the strategy, he knows that his individual contribution is valued and that the leadership has extended him trust in reaching his goals. As trust is extended from the organization to the individual, it is reciprocated and will continue until one of the parties fail to be worthy of the trust bestowed.

**Aligning job descriptions:** When strategy is cascaded down to the individual job description, it makes the trust bestowed on the individual real and measurable.

**Aligning performance review:** Nelson (1986) concluded that, "You get what you reward." Many strategy implementations initially have a big hype but fizzle out over time without any significant sustainable change in an individual's behavior. Trust is built when the organization sticks to its plan and values the contribution entrusted to each individual to such an extent that he or she is being held accountable for his or her performance. At this stage, the individual knows his trust was not misguided and that the organization has actually been worthy of his trust in the process by holding him accountable. Significant trust is built when the leader aligns the individual's performance review with the strategy. It emphasizes the perception that the leader is serious about getting everyone on board.

**Recognition and rewards:** People feel valued when the leader recognizes them for their efforts to align with the strategy and rewards them for achieving the new results. These actions build trust in the leader. The leader also builds trust if he or she leads by example during the implementation. The focus should be on the following:

- **Transparency:** Few actions erode trust like a lack of transparency. Those impacted by the change, directly or indirectly, develop trust in the leader when they experience transparency. Trust violations over time will not only erode the trust but will put the strategy in jeopardy.

- **Engaging:** People want to make a positive contribution. By engaging people not only in the problem but in the development of the solution, the leader extends trust to all stakeholders. Trust extended is trust returned. As trust is extended and returned through engagement and information sharing, strategy implementation speeds up.

- **Syndicating:** A positive perception of the leader develops when ideas are syndicated and assumptions validated. This is achieved by engaging people one level at a time, sharing ideas, and refining concepts. Syndication minimizes surprises and builds trust.

- **Collaborating:** Collaboration is important because it allows individuals to seek and discover solutions to the changes the strategy calls for. Individuals develop trust in their leader when they can collaboratively participate in the strategy development and implementation.

- **Communicating:** Well-coordinated, nonconflicting, and purposeful communication builds significant trust in the leader as it reduces confusion and adds clarity. The leader's verbal messages play an important role in building trust during an implementation. It is of utmost importance that public and private statements are aligned. When people develop a perception that the leaders hold one view publicly and another privately, confusion is created and trust is eroded. Perception needs to be clearly communicated from the leader to all impacted individuals.

- **The intent of the strategy:** The intent of the strategy and its expected results is one of the most basic elements of trust in strategy implementation. All stakeholders need to know that the intent is for the good of all. Leaders sometime fall victim to a perception that the intent is ultimately for the good of the leader alone (e.g., that he is going to retire in a year and get a golden handshake, and that he won't care what happens to the organization afterward). Only when the intent of the strategy is to benefit the organization and everybody in it will trust be built.

- **Clarification of actions:** Those impacted by the strategy will likely participate in several activities. Trust is built when they are fully aware of the purpose and the intended outcome of the activities, and they experience trust extended to them during the changes.

- **Share openly:** Few experiences erode trust faster than gossip. This can be mitigated through providing access to key information. The perception of competence and intent are shaped by the actions and words of the leader. If the leader is perceived as trustworthy through his words and actions and is willing and able to extend trust to all impacted individuals, momentum is built and individuals will adapt strategy-related behavior more effectively.

## Trust in the Solution

Trust in the leader does not necessarily transfer to trust in the solution. The executives designing the solution have the responsibility to ensure that they enable those impacted to develop trust in the solution. Trust is developed through the following activities:

**Engagement:** Not every person in an organization is asked to participate in all aspects of strategy implementation. However, as the strategy is implemented, significant engagement is seen as trust extended from management. As more trust is extended, the process becomes more interactive and participatory. This creates more opportunities for trust to be developed. At the least, every individual impacted should participate and be engaged in identifying personal and team behaviors that need to change in order to be aligned with the new strategy. They should also be engaged in developing their new behaviors through significant sponsoring by their supervisors.

**Share information:** The details of the solution become available as the strategy unfolds. Time spent building trust is significantly reduced when information is shared across the organization as it becomes available. The available information will allow the individual to select the information needed to develop trust. It is paramount to manage the information that is being shared in the organization because poorly designed or contradictory communication can undo earned trust.

**Experimentation:** When an organization asks people to change their day-to-day activities in order to bring a new strategy to fruition, they need the opportunity to experiment with the new behavior. Trust builds when the newly designed solution produces the expected results. Experimentation with the solution may not deliver all the expected results but may provide enough information to develop trust in the solution.

**Verification of assumptions and results:** Most solutions are based on a few assumptions. Trust develops when the assumptions are made visible and people are provided with the opportunity to validate them. Validated assumptions build trust, and when assumptions are proven as invalid, the solution can be adjusted, building trust in the process.

The potential of a successful strategy implementation increases significantly when those impacted by the strategy have trust in the leader and the solution. However, it is also important that the individual has internal trust, believing he or she has the skills and abilities to be successful as he or she adopts the new behavior.

## Self-Trust

A successful and sustainable change pivots on the personal belief of ability. People will evaluate themselves in light of the new demands and determine whether they trust themselves to be successful. Experimentation will allow the person to verify personal skills and abilities and build self-trust.

**Experimentation:** The intent of the experimentation is not only to verify the solution but to determine or verify that those impacted by the change have the skills and abilities to make the changes successfully. The more they succeed during experimentation, the more comfortable they become with the changes, and the faster the implementation can proceed.

**Sponsorship:** The sponsor plays a significant role in the development of those impacted by the strategy. The sponsor needs to create the opportunity for the impacted individuals to collaborate, discover, and participate in the development of the solutions. If there is a skills gap, the sponsor should be responsive and provide the needed training. Self-trust will continue to grow when those impacted receive effective sponsorship during the transition.

**Skills development:** Experimentation leads to the discovery of the skills gaps and the subsequent learning needs. Sponsorship supports the individual by creating training opportunities. However, it is the individual's responsibility to take full advantage of the skill development program.

A combined experience of experimentation, effective sponsorship, and skill development will lead to the development of self-trust. To have trust in the leader, solution, and self are critical elements.

## Trust in Others

A new strategy often impacts most employees in an organization. Individuals may have trust in their leader, the solution, and themselves but may not trust that the other individuals in their group or other groups in the organization are changing. There is often deep distrust and competition between the different silos in an organization, which can slow down or derail a strategy implementation.

Here are some ways for your employees to increase trust in others:

**Transparency:** As people experience their own journey through the change, they will observe whether others are doing the same. They want to know that others in the organization are making similar corrections, and they would also like to have information about how the change will impact others in the organization. By sharing the results of experimentation and change, people have access to the best practices that can be implemented along their own change journey. The strategic roadmap will also make clear whether that change is affecting everybody and if all are being held accountable to make the appropriate changes.

**Collaboration:** Identifying issues and solutions through collaboration allow the individual to see what others have done to be successful. This awareness builds trust in others within the organization.

**Cascading of the strategic drivers:** As individual job descriptions and performance reviews are adjusted, those impacted develop more trust in others because they are all accountable for supporting the strategy.

The development and implementation of a strategy in a trusting environment hold significant benefits to the leaders and the organization. Covey's research confirmed that trust lowers costs and speeds up change (Covey, 2006).

Planning during the initial stages of the strategy development provides an integrated roadmap. The main activities are well-coordinated and cost-optimized. Adherence to the roadmap is significantly increased in a trusting environment, allowing the strategy implementation to stay on track and on time. The duration of the syndication and collaboration is much shorter in a trusting environment. The availability of transparent information reduces the need for lengthy fact-finding actions by those impacted. Time is used to develop more effective solutions rather than questioning the information.

Effective corporate response to the human need for specific and sequential information allows those impacted to move faster from a point of unawareness to adoption. The process significantly reduces the need for people to go back and ask for additional information that is often skipped during traditional changes. This back-and-forward movement slows the process. This slowdown is neutralized by the sequential flow of the needed information.

The time saved preventing rework, retraining, resending of information, and rehashing lengthy discussions translate into reduced implementation cost. Employees have a job to focus on, and the less disruptive the strategy implementation, the more they can stay productive, translating to cost savings.

A trusting environment will not only benefit the implementation of a new strategy but will hold significant advantages for future significant change implementations. The key is that trust builds trust and that one successful implementation will increase the success of a future endeavor. If the organization created a culture of trust, it will benefit changes as well as operations.

Why would people change their beliefs or behaviors if they don't trust the people or the solutions they offer? People won't make the change, and even if they do, it will not be sustainable. The successful development and implementation of a new strategy pivots on the trust of those impacted. If there is little or no trust to support the change, it will not be successful.

Enabling those impacted to develop and build trust requires the creation of an environment where the individual can develop trust in the leader, solution, self, and others. This allows those impacted to experience the actions and listen to the words of the leader and sponsors in the context of a clearly-defined intent and a high level of transparency.

People prefer clear, simple, and compelling cases for change. They want to feel valued and engaged. They want to have some control over the behaviors they have to change. They appreciate rewards and recognitions for their actions. They want to see a clearly-defined roadmap and have well-designed support. This environment will enhance the individual's perception of the leader and intent of change, resulting in trust.

Trust is not a given or freely available. Trust is bestowed upon those whose actions and words instill confidence. It is the leader's responsibility to create a trusting culture through his or her actions and words.

## History in a Change-Enabling Milieu

Few executives are aware that an organizational history can torpedo a well-designed strategy. When people are asked if they would be willing to return to a diner where they ate something that gave them food poisoning, the answer is always a resounding "no." On the flipside, nobody minds going back to a restaurant where they had great food and good service for a reasonable price. In the same way, individuals are loath to put energy and effort into a strategy implementation when their effort in previous implementations did not yield results.

Strategy implementations happen regularly in organizations, as it is an integral part of running a business. The iterative process of developing and implementing strategies leaves behind a history. It is this history that will either enable the next change or inhibit it. Not paying attention to the historical path of strategy developments and implementation is not only unwise but outright dangerous and significantly increases the risk of a failed implementation.

The organizational environment can either enable the strategy or hinder it. History is one of the critical elements, together with culture, trust, expectations, communication, and sponsorship that need our attention. Evaluating the organizational history as it relates to the strategy implementation will enable the executives to identify those strengths that can be leveraged and those weaknesses that should be mitigated.

A change-enabling history is critically important because it impacts the individual's ability to develop a strong psychological connection with the strategy that is critical for adoption. It is therefore of utmost importance that the organization focuses on the history and reframes it in such a way that it will enable the individual to create the psychological connection.

Let's briefly look at the impact of history and then focus on mitigating weaknesses and leveraging opportunities. The goal is to create a change-enabling milieu and thus create an enabling history.

**History provides context:** Organizations experience different phases over time. Years of growth can be followed by recessions, expansions, organic growth, or M&As. Individuals with many years of service in the organization can often recall the organizational history in detail. Historically, organizations develop and implement cost-cutting strategies in recessionary times and expansion strategies during times of growth. Over time, the individuals in an organization start to develop a sense of what kind of strategies the organization adopts in which context.

The historical context is important because it drives, to some extent, expectations and a willingness to change. As an example, in the most recent recession most individuals expected to experience cost-cutting or belt-tightening strategies. As they understood the context, they were more willing to make the necessary changes.

Long-time employees are often effusive and spot on with their evaluation of the organizational history of strategy implementations. They label the strategies from "very successful" to "outright jokes." They might also tell you, for example, that the previous CEO created several successful changes while the current CEO has not, or vice versa. They are usually quite astute in identifying the groups that have demonstrated that they could implement changes like the IT department, and those who have not, such as HR or another department.

These historical trends are important because once the new strategy is associated with a specific trend it gets labeled, and the label has a lot of associated connotations. If a strategy is associated with a winning team, individuals have a greater willingness to participate and change. On the contrary, if the new strategy is associated with a losing trend, the impacted individuals will not only be reluctant to change but will likely try to stall and wait for the strategy to fail as predicted, without their changing their behavior.

**History enables predictions:** Workers will share their opinions willingly. Based on the history, employees will predict that if a specific executive is leading the implementation, it will fail. They predict this because of the specific track record of the executive. The prediction is also valid to the other side. Workers will predict success when executives with a great historical record lead the change.

**History shapes beliefs:** Beliefs drive behavior, and a new strategy calls for different aligned behaviors. History is one of several elements that shape individual beliefs. When individuals experienced a failed strategy implementation, they may come to the conclusion that the failure was due to the selection of the "wrong" strategy. As they become aware that the organization intends to implement a similar strategy, they will hold on to their personal belief that the new strategy will also fail, and they will not help implement or support the new strategy. This will prevent them from developing the needed psychological connection with the strategy.

**History kills by association:** You may have developed food poisoning in your neighborhood at one fast food restaurant belonging to a big chain. Chances are, however, that you will avoid a similar restaurant in a different location. When individuals say the new strategy smells like, tastes like, and looks like the strategy that failed previously, it is unlikely they will develop a psychological connection with the new strategy.

**History as a change enabler:** When an organization succeeds in developing a history of successful strategy implementations, the specific history can be leveraged to become an enabler of change. Success builds on success and individuals want to be part of a success story and do not want to be associated with a disaster.

As an organization assesses the past and identifies the elements of the history that will most likely impede the implementation of the new strategy, they need to develop specific actions to overcome the challenges.

Let me share some of the most effective actions that have stood the test of time.

**Acknowledge the past:** When the new strategy is associated with a past failure, it is important to develop a clearly defined wall between the new strategy and the historical failure. The first step in the development of the wall is to acknowledge the past. Acknowledging publicly that the new strategy is not linked to a past failure will make a significant contribution in developing the wall. The executives are sending a clear message to the impacted individuals that they are aware of the history the new strategy is associated with and are willing to make sure the new strategy implementation is dealt with differently.

**Identify the lessons learned from the past:** It is important to determine what happened during the last failed attempt. Individuals like to see that their leaders are learning from the past and that they are not just going to replicate the failure.

**Provide a different roadmap:** Compare and contrast. Share the main elements that contributed to the failure and how the new strategy is going to be different in the current implementation. Define the differences to such an extent that they are easily recognizable.

**Demonstrate the differences:** Don't make the mistake of telling the impacted individuals that the strategy implementation will be dealt with differently and then engage in the actions that sank the previous strategy. Be careful not to say one thing and revert back to old behaviors. If you developed the wall between the old and new strategies on paper, you need to demonstrate building the wall with actions. The key is to restore trust and confidence.

**Avoid assumptions:** A fundamental mistake made by so many executives is the assumption that they are familiar with the history and know how it is being viewed by all in the organization. The view of the history is determined by the lens of the observer. It is not as important how the executives see the history but how the impacted individuals view it. They are the ones who need to connect with the strategy psychologically.

**Mitigate quickly:** The history provides a significant opportunity for mitigation. Executives can assess the history and develop proactive risk-mitigation strategies. They don't have to wait until the implementation is in progress before mitigating any historical issues. It can be done in advance.

The history can be helpful in the implementation of the strategy. Organizations are encouraged to associate the new strategy with past successes. The new strategy can be framed in terms of duplicating previous successes and emulated in the way another successful project had been handled. This positive association will expedite the individual's ability to more quickly develop a psychological connection.

Organizations should not overlook the importance of its strategy-implementation history. The risk in overlooking its history is similar to that of not checking the amount of gas in your car before you embark on a long trip. In organizations that do not fully appreciate the impact of history, executives may develop a false sense of comfort, only to be surprised by its historical downfalls.

It is much more costly to repair the damage caused by a negative historical association than by mitigating it proactively.

## Expectations in a Change-Enabling Milieu

Expectations are critically important between a service provider and client. Meeting or missing client expectations can be the difference between highly satisfied customers and dissatisfied clients. There is a strong correlation between this relationship and a strategy implementation. Expectations are embedded in all relationships and need to be managed.

Expectations are also an important element of the organizational milieu. Expectations are linked to trust, history, and sponsorship. It is of utmost importance to address expectations on the individual level, seeing that it is an enabler in the development of all three connections to the strategy.

Expectations are part of the psychological contract between the organization and individual, where both make implicit promises of what they are willing to bring to the relationship. The employee offers specific services, time, and teamwork, while the organization promises financial rewards, opportunities for skill development, and a good environment. Years ago, when job security was taken for granted, the psychological contract was based on an assumption of a long-term relationship based on mutual trust and respect. These days, the dynamic has changed from a relational one to a contractual one. In a contractual relationship, there is no assumption of mutual long-term trust and less willingness to make accommodations on behalf of one another. Any change in expectations or working arrangements can easily be seen as an expectancy violation.

As described earlier, a change in strategy calls for a change in behaviors, and consequently, a change in expectations. Today there is an expectation that individuals will execute their day-to-day activities in alignment with the current strategy. However, if the strategy changes, the expectation is that the individual will adopt new behavior. The individual may have the expectation that he or she is already providing a professional service and that the organization cannot expect him or her to change how he or she is doing the job.

People have a strong tendency not to change but to stay within their comfort zone. When faced with change, they often make the incorrect inference that although other people will have to significantly change, they will not. Even when presented with a set of changes that strongly suggest otherwise, they tend to default to a set of individual expectations that they will not have to change much.

Expectancy violation occurs when an individual's experience is different from an expectation. If the food you receive is different from what you ordered, your expectations are violated.

Expectancy violation theory predicts that when a person's experience is different from his or her expectations, he or she will react in one of the following ways: If the outcome is better than the expectation, trust is built. If the outcome is worse than expected, it serves as a distraction and the individual will now turn his or her attention to the magnitude and meaning of the violation. The larger the magnitudes of the violation, the more negative the interpretation of the meaning of the violation. The individual now decides which action to take. The bigger the discrepancy and the more negative the meaning attached to the violation, the more likely it is the individual will lose trust and become defensive, thus stopping to conform to the predictive expectations. This is when the individual becomes disconnected from the strategy. All further communication and events will not be viewed with the same trust, and from now on, the individual is less open to change.

Expectations are embedded in all three of the connections that need to be established for strategy adoption to occur. When reality is not aligned with the individual's expectations it is seen as a violation, which lowers trust and engagement.

The dynamics of expectancy violation will be illustrated from the angle of a merger and acquisition. An M&A strategy is selected with a very specific intent in mind (e.g., to increase market share). This intent translates into a new business arrangement of the merging businesses ranging from coexistence to assimilation. This business arrangement necessitates a set of changes.

The organization assumes people will look at the necessary changes and develop their personal expectations in alignment with the new strategy and related changes. This is called "predictive expectations." This assumption may not always be valid, as people tend to develop their personal expectations aligned with their comfort zone and beliefs, which may not be aligned with assumed expectations. When their individually created expectations and subsequent experiences are not aligned, mistrust develops. This expectancy violation leads them to disconnect from the strategy, sending it on the road to failure.

The management of expectations and expectancy violations has a significant impact on the success or failure of any M&A strategy. It is therefore critical for an organization to identify critical expectations and deliberately manage them during the strategy implementation.

An advantage is gained when the:

- M&A is well defined in terms of the described continuum;

- consequences from the business arrangement that will influence expectations are identified;

- all expectations are deliberately managed;

- resistance is rigorously monitored in order to identify and mitigate any expectancy violations.

Expectancy violations are often part of an M&A. People often say things such as "this is not what I signed up for," or "nobody told me it was going to be this way," or even "if I knew it was going to be this way, I would never have agreed to this," and finally, "there is no future for me here, I have to move on." Expectancy violations are most likely driven by statements such as these.

In an M&A, the intent of the merger may be to increase market share through assimilation. There are subsequent consequences for the proposed structure, such as one of the existing entities will have to be absorbed and will thus disappear from view. In order for this to happen, lots of changes that will impact the employees of the absorbed business unit will have to take place.

Examples of these changes are the elimination of familiar processes and policies, such as the removal of particular signs and symbols, and a myriad of other changes. Organizations assume that people's predictive expectations will be realistic and aligned with the new strategy and business arrangement. If these predictive expectations and their potential impact on the individual are not made visible and attended to, it will produce a situation where the individual creates his or her own expectations regarding consequences, which might be inconsistent or in conflict with the reality they will encounter. When reality strikes, there is a big discrepancy between the expectation and the experience, which in turn fuels mistrust and creates a disconnect from the strategy.

If executives do not pay sufficient attention to people's tendency to create their own set of expectations, they may make the faulty assumption that everybody will understand the level of change and adoption they have to go through. By making this assumption, they do not pay adequate attention to expectations (predictive or individual) and do not effectively manage them. It is of critical importance that expectations be managed during an M&A and that mitigation strategies are developed to move the entities toward the intent of the business arrangement.

The key is to focus on the individual. In what way does the M&A expect an individual to change (predictive expectations)? On a personal level, what inferences do employees make about the scope of the change and the level of impact it will have on them? What are the perceived gains and losses? An expectancy violation occurs when the individuals' experiences during the M&A is inconsistent with the gains and losses they expected to experience. It is at this point that the individual gets disillusioned and subsequently disconnects from the situation, not making the changes necessary for the strategy to be successful.

The selection of the various M&A arrangement models, namely coexistence, assimilation, or transformation is based on sound business principles and is not under scrutiny in this book. The failure risk is correlated with the dynamics between what the organization sees as natural consequences to the change, their assumption that individuals will develop aligned expectations, and the individual's tendency to default to a position of little change, even in the face of contradictory evidence.

Communication is one of the tools an organization can use to reduce expectancy violations. The messages communicated before and during an M&A integration need to be consistent. Opportunities where people can examine and clarify exactly what they can realistically expect should be created. When there is a disconnect between the messages communicated and the direct experience of the impacted individuals, the result is personal disappointment, distrust, and failure to conform to what the M&A requires in terms of behavior (i.e., disconnecting from the strategy). In the same vein, if employees are not engaged and provided with a forum in which they can share their beliefs and expectations, they will hold on to their individually crafted expectations and experience the disconnect when things do not turn out the way they thought they would. If a significant number of individuals experience expectancy violation and subsequent disconnection, the goals of the M&A cannot be realized.

## Managing Expectations

Managing expectations is important during an M&A. Expectation management is a critical success factor because it addresses the basic needs of the individuals impacted and contributes to the creation of a change-enabling milieu.

Organizations that focus equally on all impacted individuals by not overlooking the impact of change on existing members have fewer incidents of expectancy violations. A high level of transparency contributes to fewer expectancy violations.

Organizations should prepare an expectancy violation management plan, which includes identifying and managing the predictive expectations; recognizing the critical default expectations of individuals; creating an environment where the individual's default expectations can be examined and altered; screening communications to prevent expectation violations; and assessing resistance in order to identify expectancy violations in a timely manner.

When expectation management is done well, it will become a positive and productive element of the change-enabling milieu. Managing the key expectations effectively at the individual level serves not only to enhance the individuals' connection to the strategy but facilitates the implementation and adoption of the strategy.

## Communication in a Change-Enabling Milieu

When used effectively, communication is one of the most powerful tools toward accelerating strategy implementations. On the other hand, when communication becomes ineffective it becomes a torpedo that can sink a strategy in a short time. Communication is fundamental to the change-enabling milieu. It is the vehicle that enables executives to share their concepts and ideas. It also enables interaction and engagement of all impacted individuals. Communication is also fundamental in the creation of psychological, structural, and contractual connections. Scholars in communication highlight the fact that communication is irreversible. A Russian proverb claims that "once a word goes out of your mouth, you can never swallow it again." It is also true that many organizations struggle to find a good balance between reviewing paralysis and communication without planning. One fact is clear: ineffective communication will hamper even the best strategy. During strategy implementation, impacted individuals need to move from their current day-to-day activities to a point where they have adopted behaviors that will make the new strategy effective. They need a significant amount of information, structure and support to help them make the transition.

In order to be effective, the organization needs to have a thorough understanding of the individual's need for information in order to change, and has to tailor its messages according to that need. It also needs to make sure that conflicting messages are not communicated because individuals will use the confusion as an excuse not to take action or change.

## Effective Communication Is Paramount to Strategy Implementation

Individuals and organizations communicate throughout the day. However, ineffective communication is a problem. A successful strategy implementation relies on effective communication.

Effective communication happens when audience selection is done thoughtfully. Every audience has unique characteristics and requires custom designed messages to enable the specific audience to hear the messages effectively. The purpose of effective communication is clearly defined; a specific message is developed; the most effective delivery vehicle is selected; and the message is sent at the right time. After the message has been delivered, the results are measured to ensure that the intended purpose was achieved.

The vast majority of organizations believe they are effective when communicating to all the workers in the organization. However, "post mortems" on failed strategy implementation indicate that ineffective communication contributed significantly to the failure.

It is well known that beliefs drive behaviors, and new strategies calls for new beliefs and behaviors that will achieve the planned results. The overarching measurable purpose of effective communication during strategy development and implementation is to provide the individuals impacted by the strategy the information they need to:

- Become fully aware of the strategy as it relates to the content of the business case;

- Develop a clear understanding of how the new strategy will impact them and allow them to discover their own beliefs and behaviors that need to change;

- Develop confidence in their sponsor's support to make the transition;

- Develop confidence that the new behaviors are aligned with the new strategy and will deliver the anticipated results through controlled experimentation;

- Demonstrate that the new behaviors can realize the results over time;

- Receive the rewards and recognition needed, serving as motivation during the transition;

- Adopt the new behaviors and sustain them over time.

Communication is a key tool in helping individuals connect to the strategy psychologically, unlocking their willingness to alter their behavior. Effective communication is a critical element in the change-enabling milieu and is fundamental to all the connections. Most organizations communicate effusively during a strategy implementation, and often the communication is a source of confusion rather than illuminating.

Communication is the most frequently used tool but often does not yield the intended results. The communication skills required for the implementation of a strategy is often at a much higher level than expected. The following are the deadliest communication mistakes that can be made during a strategy implementation.

- Communicating without a clear understanding of the purpose of the messages;

- Communicating without validating the message;

- Communicating through ineffective message-delivery vehicles;

- Communicating without assessing the effectiveness of the communication;

- Communicating only with sponsors (who are not the only communicators in an organization);

- Participating in the confusion trap;
- Ignoring or failing to identify critical messages.

Each of the above communication mistakes can paralyze a strategy implementation. Most failed strategy implementations get bogged down in all seven of the above-mentioned mistakes. If only one of these can derail a strategy implementation, imagine how much risk a combination of all seven present. Here they are again, in further detail.

The first mistake an organization can make is to communicate without a clear purpose. Have you ever opened an e-mail or letter and asked yourself, "Why in the world does this person want me to know this? What do I have to do with this?" Organizations send out thousands of communications every year, and often the intent is unclear. The fact is, there are only a handful of purposes behind messages. Organizations communicate because they want people to (1) do something specific (e.g., register for training); (2) stop an activity (e.g., stop using the old parking area); (3) consider an action or position (e.g., complete the open enrollment of their insurance policy); (4) develop awareness about an issue (e.g., recognize a new strategy); or (5) develop understanding around an issue (e.g., how the strategy will impact them).

If you hear statements similar to "we sent it because people want to know," "people need the information," or "we send this every month," you know that the organization is only adding a costly pile of junk mail and has not really defined the intent of the communication. The consequences of creating junk mail without a clearly defined purpose have a significant impact on strategy implementation. Some of the consequences are that individuals will ignore most of the communication and will not take appropriate action; individuals will use informal relations rather than the sponsors to clarify concepts; sponsors will not be able to sponsor all the key messages; and executives will increase the flow of information without getting the intended results.

In strategy implementation, there is interplay between the human need for information in order to adopt new behaviors and the corporate responsibility to provide the structure and information. Each of the messages sent during a strategy implementation has to have a clear intent to move people along from unawareness to adoption of the new strategy-aligned behavior. Not defining the purpose of key messages will not only inhibit effective sponsorship, it will prevent individuals from discovering their personal beliefs and behaviors that need to be adjusted in order to be aligned with the strategy. When individuals don't develop and embrace new behaviors, they will not forge a psychological connection with the strategy, or if a connection has been established, they will disconnect from the strategy and bring the implementation to a near halt.

Another important consequence is that the executives are unable to measure the effectiveness of their communication. When they notice that the strategy implementation is losing traction, they tend to increase the flow of information, again without clearly specifying the intent, adding to the complexity of the problem.

This problem is avoided if the organization has a clear understanding of individuals' need for specific information in order to change, and the specific intent of every message is defined and clarified before the message is crafted. If organizations consistently ask what they want to achieve and what they want the audience to do before crafting the message, this mistake can be avoided. When a clear intent is defined, it can be measured to see whether the message realized the intent. It will also significantly reduce the amount of communication needed to be successful.

The second mistake is communicating without validating the message. How often have you heard, "Who sent that out?" or "They didn't check with me," or "They have to send a clarification of that?" These statements are symptomatic of an inadequate communication plan.

Let's look at the following example. AAV Pharmaceuticals is implementing a new strategy. The senior management team is responsible for the implementation. AAV's structure is a complex matrix. The chief marketing officer (CMO) sends out information related to the strategy that is slightly different from what the chief operating officer (COO) sent out. Tom Black, the rep in the Phoenix store, thus receives two conflicting messages. This happens daily in most organizations.

The CMO and the COO didn't validate that the information was synchronized, clear, and aligned. The consequences of this deadly mistake have a significant impact on the implementation of the strategy. The consequences are that the messages have to be retracted, refined, and resent, and sponsors will not be able to understand messages as long as they are not in agreement with one another.

The most significant consequence is that individuals become aware of these disagreements and conclude that the leaders are not on the same page, and therefore, they wait for executive leadership to sort it out before taking any action. People know from experience that changes will not effectively be sponsored as long as there are disagreements among the leaders. Even if changes are made, they will not be sustainable until agreement is reached. This hesitation will slow the strategy implementation, and if enough of these situations occur, no change will take place and the strategy won't be implemented.

This problem can be avoided through a process change in the communication plan. The most effective way to avoid this is with a brief validation process that consists of a few steps where executives share all the strategy-related communication with one another before they communicate it with the rest of the organization.

One way to accomplish this is to post all strategy-related messages on a limited-access bulletin board for twenty-four hours before it is communicated. This enables the executives or their staffs to screen messages and ensure that conflicting messages are not transmitted. This is a cost-effective solution mitigating a deadly communication problem.

The third mistake is to communicate without assessing its effectiveness. I frequently ask sponsors, "How do you know there is water in an old open well?" Invariably they reply, "Just throw a rock into the well." That is true, but it is not the act of throwing the rock into the well that gives us the information. It is the splashing—the returning sound—that provides the answer. You can even figure out the depth of the well by calculating the lapse in time from throwing the rock to hearing the return sound. The point is that it is not the art of throwing rocks that will tell you whether people heard you but the art of listening to their response.

One of the deadliest mistakes in organizational communication is to send communications to several audiences and not have a structured process in place to measure the effectiveness of the communication. It is a myth to think people hear you or listen when you speak. Organizations operating under the assumption that they just have to communicate without measuring the effectiveness will experience difficulty implementing any strategy.

When an organization does not determine the effectiveness of their communication, they will have little sense of where the organization is in relation to the strategy. The normal informal feedback from the organization to the executives adds to this complexity. Informal feedback is traditionally very positive or very negative. Executives may conclude that their progress is somewhere in the middle and develop a false sense of security.

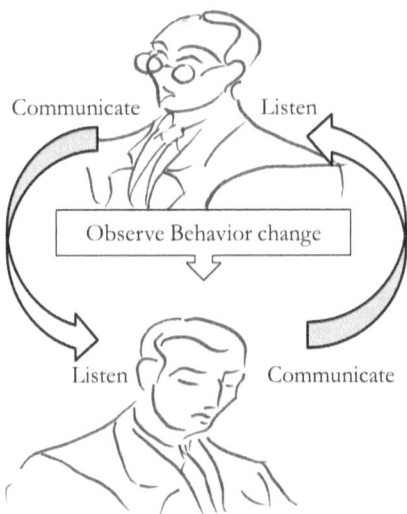

*Figure 2.1. Communication Flow*

Avoiding this problem necessitates a two-pronged approach. First, clearly define the purpose of the communication. Articulate what you want the audience to do before the messages are communicated. Second, develop an independent internal validation process. Contact the targeted audience and assess to what degree they acted in the way the messages called for. It is important to create a valid sample size in order to measure the effectiveness accurately. Observing behavior is a better measure of effectiveness than verbal reporting.

If the data indicates that the communication was not effective, stop the flow of communication and spend time identifying the cause of the ineffective communication. Most organizations just resend the information, resulting in the same ineffectiveness.

Another mistake is when sponsors are not the only communicators. When it comes to changing, people should only listen to their sponsors because their sponsors are the ones who measure their performance and determine their future in the organization. If messages are received from a variety of sources, confusion results. For a strategy change to be sustainable, all strategy-related messages need to come from the sponsors.

When AAV Pharmaceuticals implemented their growth strategy, individual reps received calls and instructions from both the marketing and financial departments. However, the information and the instructions they received from their supervisors were slightly different. The reps were bombarded with different goals, metrics, expectations, and instructions to follow, all under the umbrella of the strategy. These conflicting messages triggered resistance from the reps.

People have the tendency to ignore any request for change when they receive mixed messages from different sources. We often hear remarks similar to "They don't know what they are doing"—referring to the executives.

The consequences of mixed messages on the strategy implementation are significant. Situations are exploited by individuals resisting the change. They will share these conflicting messages with any person willing to listen. They will add to the confusion by pulling others into the mix. They will also state that they will not change until they are confident the executives know what they are doing. Their reaction will slow the strategy implementation down to the level where it is at risk of failure.

The solution for this is to have the sponsor be the deliverer of the key messages. Even if subsequent departments want to communicate to AAV Pharmaceutical's Phoenix rep, Tom Black, they have to do it through Tom's supervisor. Creating a clearinghouse mechanism where all messages are screened for consistency further mitigates this problem.

Participating in the confusion trap is a deadly communication mistake that happens all too often. A confusion trap is an effective manifestation of resistance to change. I observed this at Manchester College (North Manchester, Indiana), where I served as an adjunct. A week before the students had to hand in a term paper, a student who had not yet started the paper raised his hand and said he was confused about the paper he had to prepare. His intent was to get an extension. The last thing an instructor wants is to create confusion, so she started clarifying the intent and purpose of the paper. The more information the instructor provided, the more the student told her that he was getting even more confused. Within a minute, other students raised their hands and told her they first thought they understood but now were also confused. How could she expect them to prepare the paper if they were confused? She had to postpone the due date in an effort to clarify the topic. The student was successful in his goal of getting an extension through the creation of the confusion trap and the instructor's inability to spot it and act accordingly.

When people do not want to do something or want to change their behavior, they may tell their supervisor they are confused, because they have

45

learned that if they say they are confused, they don't have to spend any energy trying to change. The supervisor will go into overdrive trying to clarify the issue and spend his or her energy explaining. Eventually, the supervisor will run out of energy and become unable to sponsor the change. A net result is that the individuals who participated in the confusion trap do not change anything, and the supervisor gives up and moves on to the next project. This is a clear home run for the change-resistant individuals.

Consequently, when sponsors don't identify a confusion trap they will participate in it, burning valuable energy and stalling the strategy. If a series of these situations occur, there is an increased risk that the sponsor will lose interest and not sponsor the change, which can have significant implications for the strategy implementation.

To avoid a confusion trap the sponsor must have the skills and knowledge to recognize the trap. As soon as the sponsor identifies the trap, the focus needs to be turned back on the "confused" individual. Let the individual spend the energy clarifying the confusion. Ask the individual to review all the FAQs (frequently asked questions) to determine exactly where the confusion is.

Applying the above practice can have several positive effects: sponsors don't expend valuable energy; the individual spends personal energy on self-education; and if the individual points to a real issue, the sponsor can take effective steps in mitigating the issue. The biggest risk here is in not identifying the trap and falling into it. It is most effective if this topic is addressed during formal sponsor development, where they can be given the opportunity to practice and develop their trap-avoiding skills.

The next mistake happens when strategy communication is not distinctly "branded." On my way home in the afternoon, I pick up my mail. Once at home, I screen the mail. I automatically sort the mail: junk mail, credit card solicitations, advertising, and the important stuff. Anything unimportant will end up in the recycle bin in a second. I will only pay attention to information I consider important.

A similar story unfolds in organizations. Individuals arrive at the office, check their e-mails and other mail, and within a second discard information deemed useless or unimportant. This selection process is natural behavior for all of us.

In a strategy implementation, this natural behavior can lead to the following significant consequences:

• Critical information will be discarded;

- Targeted audiences will be uninformed;
- Information will penetrate targeted audiences inconsistently, creating confusion leading to mistrust;
- Sponsors become ineffective.

The above can slow down any strategy implementation. If sponsors cannot sponsor the changes, the strategy implementation is at risk. This problem is avoided by thorough "branding" of all strategy-related messages. This is accomplished by using a specific look and format for all messages. Branding allows all impacted individuals to recognize the messages and make an informed decision to either read or discard it. It is the sponsor's responsibility to ensure their messages are clearly identifiable by the intended audiences.

Effective communication is pivotal to the success of any strategy implementation. Internal communication is one of the most embedded practices in organizations. Over time, an organization develops communication habits that may not be effective enough to be helpful in a strategy implementation. Organizations face seven deadly communication-related mistakes during a strategy implementation: (1) communicating without a clear understanding of the purpose of the messages, (2) communicating without validating the message, (3) communicating through ineffective message-delivery vehicles, (4) communicating without assessing the effectiveness of the communication, (5) communicating only with sponsors (who are not the only communicators in an organization), (6) participating in the confusion trap, and (7) ignoring or failing to identify critical messages. Avoiding these deadly communication traps is based on the carpenter's principle: measure twice, cut once. Organizations need to get down to the basic principles of organizational communication to become effective communicators.

To sum up: Before communicating, determine the purpose and what the results need to be. Brand the message in such a way that all impacted individuals will understand it to be an important message. Ensure all the sponsors are on the same page and are sending out aligned messages by creating a communication "clearinghouse." Hold sponsors responsible for all communication to their subordinates; do not delegate this task. Once a message has been delivered, measure its effectiveness by determining if the appropriate actions were taken.

Effective communication is an essential ingredient of the change-enabling milieu. It facilitates the flow of information and is the main ingredient in establishing the three critical connections needed for a successful strategy implementation.

## Sponsorship in a Change-Enabling Milieu

Sponsorship is defined as one who assumes responsibility for someone or something. Organizational leaders sponsor many activities as part of their leadership role and, as such, the concepts of leadership and sponsorship have become almost synonymous. Yet there is a world of difference between the role of the leader and that of a sponsor.

Sponsorship is arguably the most important element of the change-enabling milieu. Employees who receive effective sponsorship are much more likely to connect psychologically to the strategy. Sponsorship is responsible for supporting the individual in making the necessary connections as well as for creating the structural and contractual connections that can be seen as an organizational focus. Despite the critical role of sponsorship, many organizations are loath to invest in sponsorship development. In this section, we will look at the critical role of sponsorship, what it is, how to be a sponsor, and how to avoid its associated pitfalls.

Executives at the helm of organizations are leaders. They reached the executive level due to their leadership abilities and skills. We find libraries filled with books dissecting leadership from all angles. There is no shortage of leadership workshops and seminars addressing all dimensions of leadership. People want to be known as leaders and want to be acknowledged for their specific leadership styles, and most leaders work hard to refine their leadership practices. Leadership is important.

The leader is the person in front, spearheading the way, breaking the ground, setting the direction for others to follow. The leader is the person with the skills to rally people and focus their attention in a specific direction. The most successful leaders have large numbers of followers who embrace the leader's beliefs and adopt behaviors aligned with his vision. Abandoning the leader has little consequence to the follower because that following was done voluntarily.

Someone may follow the president and embrace him as a leader. That individual will support him by writing a check, attending his rallies, and defending his policies and actions. If the president urges people to buy only American brands, that individual may vow to buy only an American-brand vehicle. In this way, individuals may change behaviors to support their leader.

Should the president do or say something that is misaligned with their personal beliefs, individuals have the choice to stop following him. They may choose to stop their financial contributions and verbal support. They can withdraw their support without obvious consequences. Not supporting the president will most likely not cost them their jobs or any financial consequences.

Sponsorship is not the same as leadership. Is there a difference between leadership and sponsorship? Are all leaders not sponsors? Why should I be a sponsor if I am a leader? Why should I develop sponsorship if I develop leadership? What is wrong with the "change-management people"? Why do they keep referring to sponsorship?

These are all valid questions. As an immigrant, I never heard about sponsorship until I came to the United States in the mid-90s. A staff member at the US consul asked me, "Who is your sponsor?" What I didn't realize was that I couldn't immigrate to the United States without a sponsor. The staff member explained that the sponsor is the person responsible for underwriting my application, for providing a guarantee on my behalf.

The sponsor is the guarantor, backer, supporter, or promoter, the person helping others achieve their goals. I like to think of the sponsor as the person cosigning my immigration application. I quickly learned that there is a significant difference between a sponsor and a leader. As the sponsor cosigned my immigration application, I noted that he added a few powerful rules and conditions in the process. Suddenly I had to make the choice of adhering to the rules or suffering significant consequences.

Let me say it again. I was voluntarily accepting the conditions imposed by the sponsor, because otherwise he would not sponsor my application and I would not be able to immigrate. I ran into a contract where I had to act in a specific way to receive the intended outcome.

Sponsorship is the personal service of engaging with the impacted individuals to define and quantify the new behaviors the strategy calls for. The sponsor facilitates the process of the individual committing to the behavior changes and solidifies the expectations and consequences in a contractual agreement.

49

Sponsorship is not leadership. Sponsorship is a personal service of engaging with direct reports and guiding them to define and quantify the new behaviors the strategy calls for. The sponsor facilitates the process of the individual committing to the behavior changes and solidifies the expectations and the consequences in a contractual agreement. The sponsor is ultimately responsible for enforcing the process and consequences.

Management focuses on organizational operations, encompassing a wide scope of activities without a limit on the duration, whereas sponsorship is focused on a specific and limited-scope activity within a limited time frame. Sponsorship focuses on a specific project that is not yet operational but is expected to become fully operational in the future.

Once the project is complete and the activities become operational, it becomes management's responsibility. In an operational environment, the three basic connections already exist, and the manager has to sustain the connections while in a sponsoring environment. The sponsor is responsible for creating the change-enabling milieu and making the connections. We can conclude that sponsorship is a subset of management.

Sponsorship is more closely aligned with management than with leadership. Where leadership is forward thinking, motivating, and has a big-picture focus, management and sponsorship have to do with how to get something done. Management is concerned with planning and organizing projects and operations; allocating resources to minimize costs and maximize benefits; directing practices and procedures; establishing controls to measure the effectiveness and efficiencies; and motivating subordinates. Management is concerned with activities and the immediate results of those activities.

Sponsorship is fundamentally responsible for creating the change-enabling milieu and the three connections, whereas management has to do with maintenance. Creating and maintaining these elements are very different from one another.

Creating the change-enabling milieu requires the sponsor to assess and adjust the critical elements—namely culture, history, expectations, trust, and communication. The sponsor is the one who facilitates the creation of the three critical connections. He or she provides the individual with the sequential information and structure needed to create the psychological connection. Individuals and their sponsors integrate the strategy into the business-planning process and discover the details of the required behavior change in the structural connection. The sponsor is the person who anchors the behavior changes in the contractual connection.

Maintaining the critical connections requires monitoring, providing rewards, and enforcing selective consequences as long as the current strategy is active. Management focuses on all dimensions over a wide scope of activities without a limit on the duration, whereas a sponsorship is focused on a specific and limited scope activity within a limited time frame. Sponsorship focuses on a specific project, and the minute the project is complete and the activities become operational, it becomes a management responsibility.

A sponsor expects specific behaviors from individuals who are aligned with the strategy. A sponsor engages those impacted individuals and defines their behaviors. A sponsor and the individual identify the success criteria and the rewards. The "golden rule of sponsorship" is to reward individuals for sustaining the behavior designed collaboratively with the sponsor. Sponsorship is a service of support and reward.

Sponsorship plays a very specific role. We all have a repertoire of roles we play. Sometimes we are a parent, caregiver, sports fan, boss, leader, volunteer, and more. All of these roles are different and require a different approach to be successful.

We don't focus in this section on the role of the leader but on the role of the sponsor, recognizing that individuals can play more than one role. Leaders can play the role of sponsor and vice versa.

Let's look in more detail at the importance of sponsorship, its effectiveness, and how to develop sponsorship.

## Why Sponsorship Is Important

Sponsors serve as the glue between the horizontal and vertical layers in an organization. As stated previously, sponsorship is a subset within the management role. The sponsorship role is always of limited duration. It starts during strategy development and lasts until realization. As the implementation unfolds, the sponsor helps and supports his or her direct reports. The sponsor builds trust in the strategy, manages expectations, and engages all impacted direct reports. The sponsor holds the group together and ensures the creation and maintenance of the three critical connections. If sponsorship fails, all three critical connections may be affected.

**Sponsors distribute information:** Individuals don't care to receive information from an array of sources. When the information impacts them personally in terms of what they do, the content of their job description, or rewards, they want to hear it directly from their supervisors. Whereas a change in strategy calls for a change in behavior, it becomes critical that all the information comes from the direct sponsors of the strategic changes. Sponsorship is thus important because it communicates all the information to the impacted individuals.

**Sponsors monitor the pulse of the implementation:** Sponsors have unique access to their direct reports and to others. This access may be through formal or informal relationships and puts the sponsor in an ideal position to measure the quality of the three critical connections and the change-enabling milieu. The sponsor can also detect any adoption risk and initiate risk mitigation strategies. Due to the position of the sponsors in the organization, they serve as a valuable source of information.

**Sponsors create a change-enabling milieu:** The sponsor is responsible for adjusting the current milieu to a change-enabling milieu by assessing the culture, trust, history, and communication and then adjusting everything to facilitate the implementation.

**Sponsors provide direction:** Change elevates the unknown and uncertainty. People in general are wary of the unknown, and it is no different during a strategy implementation. The sponsor is in the best position to provide direction and can shed light on the strategy and actions needed to bring it to fruition. He or she can reduce some of the uncertainty through sharing information and providing direct support.

## What Is Effective Sponsorship?

Sponsorship is a personal management service provided by the leader to his or her direct reports. Remember that sponsorship has a specific focus for a set period of time. The impacted individuals need support during the transition stages of the strategy.

What are the most significant services a sponsor can provide to direct reports during the implementation of the strategy?

**Time:** A new strategy calls for a change in behavior. Individuals will spend significant time articulating specific aligned-behavior changes. They have to develop confidence that their sponsor is in agreement with the identified behavior changes. All potential discrepancies need to be discussed and clarified. It is, therefore, of utmost importance that the sponsor allocates sufficient time to discuss it in detail. Time allocation demonstrates the sponsor's commitment to the strategy. The allocation of personal time to the strategy increases the level of sponsorship significantly.

**Resources:** Most strategic changes consume significant resources. The resource needs often include training, skills, competency development, and development time. As employees identify the necessary changes, the sponsor needs to identify the resource needs. Any hesitation from the sponsor in allocating sufficient resources will create doubt about the importance of the strategy in the minds of direct reports. Effective sponsorship does not mean that any and all requests for resources are approved; at the minimum, the sponsor needs to stay engaged in the process of determining appropriate resources. Building and meeting resources through collaboration will significantly enhance the effectiveness of the sponsor.

**Public support:** The initiating and supporting sponsors have to be the main communicators promoting the strategy. Individuals have an expectation that all sponsors will publicly support the strategy and associated changes. Sponsors should leverage public events to demonstrate their support for the new strategy.

**Private support:** Sponsors are vulnerable when it comes to private conversations. Just think of the tremendous implications when a sponsor verbally supports the strategy during an internal staff meeting. The staff will be energized by the sponsor's enthusiasm. What will happen if the same sponsor joins a few staff members for dinner and expresses concern about the strategy? News that the sponsor is not fully supportive of the strategy will spread like wildfire, and staff will not connect with the strategy, or, if previously connected, they will disconnect from the strategy.

Few things can derail a strategy implementation as fast as when sponsors' public statements and private comments about the strategy are misaligned. Sponsorship effectiveness increases as private and public discourse stays aligned.

**Rewards and recognition:** Sponsorship becomes more effective when the sponsor aligns rewards with the required strategy-aligned behavior. Individuals will experiment with the new behaviors, and well-designed recognition will encourage the adoption of the new behaviors. As the new behaviors produce results, it is of utmost importance to ensure that the behaviors are rewarded.

**Consequences:** Sponsors can undo strategy implementations in a split second when they don't apply any consequences when individuals do not adopt the new strategy. What is the value of a new strategy implementation when there are no consequences for success or failure? The effectiveness of sponsorship is hampered by the lack of willingness by the sponsor or the organization to apply consequences as needed.

Effective sponsorship is a service to those impacted by the changes the new strategy calls for. It should not be a burden but a privilege to be a sponsor of a strategy implementation.

## *Recognizing Effective Sponsorship*

Effective sponsorship is evident in the sustained behavior changes of those reporting to the sponsor. Those changes will not occur or be sustained without effective sponsorship. The direct causal relationship between sponsorship and behavior changes have been studied for years. Typically, behavior change lasts as long as its sponsorship lasts.

Based on the premise that beliefs drive behaviors and sponsorship is a set of behaviors, we should start looking at the beliefs about sponsorship. Through interviewing a significant number of successful sponsors over the years, a common belief that "a leader leads by example" surfaced. How philosophically we wish to view this statement is open for discussion, but one thing is clear: people are significantly more impacted by your actions than your words.

The effectiveness of sponsorship is determined by the sponsor's direct reports, his peers, and his supervisor. Let's briefly look at sponsorship from these angles and how the triangulation provides us with significant insight into sponsorship.

**Subordinates** experience effective sponsorship service when sponsors:

- Identify and address subordinates' needs for structured information and support in order to embrace the required change.

- Develop cascading sponsorship to the lowest individual level.

- Blend the design of the intended desired state with their need for information and structure to change.

- Provide the information and structure with the specific purpose of moving them from a state of unawareness to adoption of the new strategy-required behaviors.

- Provide sufficient personal time to participate in key aspects of the strategy design and implementation.
- Allocate sufficient resources for them to be successful.
- Align public and private comments.
- Leverage rewards, recognition, and consequences.
- Keep the realization metric on the radar until reached.
- Are transparent.

**Peers** experience effective sponsorship when sponsors:
- Identify and address their needs, enabling collaboration.
- See reports and evidence that their peers' subordinates view them as effective sponsors.
- Change behavior and strategy to impact people outside their direct reporting lines; issues are effectively escalated to the appropriate level in the organization. This is the ability to develop sponsorship upward in the organization.
- Value input from their peers.

**Supervisors** view their direct reports as effective sponsors when:
- A high level of thoughtfulness and detail is evident in the design of the strategy or change.
- Consequences are well-defined and mechanisms deployed to uncover and mitigate unattended consequences effectively.
- A sound change-management plan is deployed, optimizing communication, learning, and rewards tools.
- There is a high level of transparency and accountability.
- They are viewed by their peers and subordinates as effective sponsors.
- The intended outcomes of the strategy or change are achieved within the time and resources allocated.

## *Recognizing Ineffective Sponsorship*

Although ineffective sponsorship is technically the flipside of effective sponsorship, it is more challenging to recognize. Organizations get bombarded with strategy-related feedback from different angles for different reasons, fueled by conscious and unconscious motives. This feedback is further intertwined with feedback associated with day-to-day operations. Organizations often develop a strategy-related issues log but seldom make the connection between the myriad issues and sponsorship.

The link between strategy-implementation issues and sponsorship is sometimes not recognized because the information is often deflected. The reason for this is because sponsorship is a personal service, and sponsors will deflect information in order not to be exposed. Nobody wants to look bad in front of others or be told they are not providing a good service, so they avoid this through the natural tendency to deflect. When issues manifest over time, people use this natural deflecting tendency and frame the issues in a context other than their own skills and competencies. Although this is natural behavior, it complicates the organization's ability to distinguish between sponsorship-related issues and other issues.

Sponsorship is pivotal to the success of any strategy or change. It is paramount to ensure strong effective sponsorship during the duration of the strategy or change implementation.

A few sponsorship myths also add to the complexity of identifying ineffective sponsorship. Let's look briefly at a few.

**You can be an effective sponsor even though you may still have unanswered questions.** In reality, it is not realistic to expect effective-change sponsorship when the sponsor still has personal doubts about the change. Can a sponsor direct his subordinates to adopt new behaviors and part with old behaviors when he is not yet convinced? Effective sponsorship is not a continuous service but stops and starts in a matter of minutes every day for the duration of the project. It comes to a grinding halt every time the sponsor experiences doubt about the change or his issues surrounding it have not been addressed. An effective sponsor is proactive and seeks information to address his own doubts to minimize the occurrence and duration of the stops and starts in order to keep momentum.

**Being appointed makes you an effective sponsor.** This is also a myth, as we have previously indicated. Sponsorship is a service and a specific set of behaviors, not a title. Someone can be appointed sponsor of a strategy, but unless the individual provides the personal sponsorship services to his or her direct reports, he or she is not a sponsor of the change. Data from failed strategies or changes points to an "appointed sponsor," who then delegated the sponsorship role and responsibilities to others, and in the process, set the stage for failure. This "delegation" of sponsorship results in "blame game comments" when the strategy is derailed and nobody accepts personal responsibility for the lack of sponsorship.

**Once an effective sponsor, always an effective sponsor.** Sponsorship is situational. People tend to forget that the sponsor, as a person, is as exposed to the new strategy or change as any of his or her subordinates. The sponsor has to deal with his own issues before he can become an effective sponsor. Furthermore, as beliefs drive behavior, every strategy or change engages a different set of beliefs and should be treated as a singular event. One of the cardinal sins of sponsorship is to appoint a previously effective sponsor of a strategy or change implementation as a sponsor with the assumption that he or she will be an effective sponsor again.

**Sponsorship is transferable.** Sponsorship is a very personal service. It is inevitable that supporting sponsors may get sick, promoted, or may move on to a next assignment before the strategy is implemented. The organization cannot assume that the incoming person will pick up the slack and automatically be an effective sponsor. Every time a sponsor is replaced, the organization must develop the new incumbent to become an effective sponsor of the strategy. The result of not addressing this effectively is always the same—a big black hole where information from the top is absorbed and no meaningful direction is provided to the direct reports of the new sponsor. This results in confusion and stagnation, putting the implementation at serious risk. Sponsorship is not transferable.

**We don't need sponsorship development, we know what to do.** If this statement was true, why is the success rate of M&As only 53 percent? Who will invest money in a fund where the risk of losing the total investment is 47 percent and the probability of gaining any return only 17 percent? Why run the risk? Allocating resources to develop strong sponsors in the organization will yield a significant return when strategies and changes are successfully implemented.

**Sponsorship is elevated and in the job descriptions.** Through studying post mortems of failed strategy implementations, it was discovered that sponsorship as a competency was seldom mentioned in a job description, or, when mentioned, was not inadequately defined or ever measured. This contrasts with the practice that almost 50 percent of an executive's day-to-day activities are related to strategy or change. It may be hard to connect all the dots, but people get assessed and compensated based on the line items in their job descriptions. Given these facts, no wonder so many strategy implementations are at risk or fail to yield the anticipated results.

The effectiveness of the sponsorship should be assessed using 360-degree feedback. The assessment will flush out those issues that may impede the strategy implementation and will provide focus areas for sponsorship development at individual and organizational levels.

## Cascading Sponsorship

**Initiating sponsor:** Developing and cascading sponsorship goes hand-in-hand. It all starts with the person with "the keys"—meaning the highest-level person in the organization with the responsibility to decide whether a strategy is moving forward or has to be shut down. How is this initiating sponsor identified? Daryl R. Conner, in his book, *Managing at the Speed of Change*, wrote: A sponsor is the individual or group who has the power to sanction or legitimize change. However, it is also done by looking at those who will be impacted. Remember, those impacted want to receive sponsorship from their direct supervisors. Who is the common denominator, the one person linked to those impacted? That person will become the primary sponsor, and the rest of the cascading leadership become supporting sponsors.

A visualization of cascading sponsorship is that of a chain, anchored in the boardroom, hanging to the bottom levels of the organization. If the intent of the strategy is to let all individuals linked down to the last shackle change their behavior, then it is imperative that all the shackles stay intact. If one shackle disconnects, the strategy will be at risk until the shackle gets reconnected. New strategies call for new behaviors, and without cascading sponsorship to every level where new behaviors are needed, the strategy will disconnect and fail.

One should not make the assumption that the sponsor chain is always intact. Every person is not automatically a sponsor, so the chain does not automatically exist. We need to take two actions: first, develop every person responsible to play the role of sponsor and link them to one another to create the chain; and second, monitor the intactness of the chain, because sponsors will disconnect the chain for a thousand different reasons.

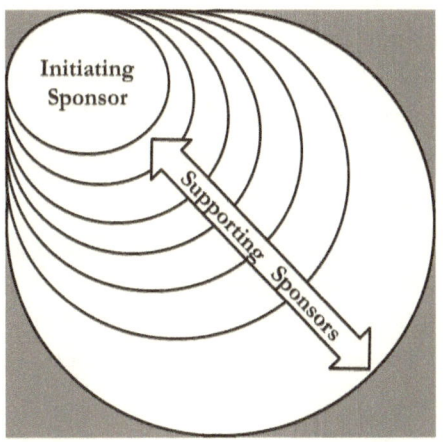

*Figure 2.2. Initiating and Supporting Sponsors*

**Supporting sponsors:** Sponsorship lives in the moment and can fluctuate in seconds. Effective sponsorship is negatively impacted every time the sponsor encounters activities or messages that are conflicting with his or her personal beliefs, values, or expectations. The sponsor becomes, for a brief period, "paralyzed" and cannot be an effective sponsor. This brief pause comes at the expense of effectiveness. This is not impacting the ability or willingness to be an effective sponsor but is analogous to stopping and taking a pebble out of your shoe. This interrupted forward motion is not only normal, it's natural. However, if an adequate level of sponsorship service cannot be provided to the individual, more and more of these brief stops will take place, which will eventually slow the momentum of the implementation, as well as the sustainability thereof.

Sustainable sponsorship has two distinct focus areas: the proactive focus and the monitoring focus. The initiating sponsor's ability to develop sponsorship at all levels of the organization proactively is the key to creating effective and sustainable sponsorship for the complete strategy implementation. The initiating sponsor has to identify and mitigate potential obstacles that may impede people in becoming supporting sponsors. Additionally, the initiating sponsor is required to monitor supporting sponsorship by using sponsorship-assessment tools at predetermined points during the life cycle of the strategy implementation. This monitoring creates sustainability.

Sustained sponsorship is a reflection of how well the organization developed and monitored sponsorship. As the monitoring process detects challenges, the organization needs to address them as effectively as possible to ensure continued sponsorship. The faster a sponsorship problem can be detected and fixed, the smoother the experience. This is analogous to traveling by car during Thanksgiving weekend. You don't fill the car with fuel and hit the road and ignore the fuel level the rest of the weekend. You will only have an event-free experience if you monitor the gas level and refuel as needed and available. You don't wait until you run out of gas and then get mad or disappointed because the vehicle stopped. How much time and effort will it take to get going again? In the same way, you have to fill your strategy implementation with sponsorship and check it regularly during the trip, or you may get stranded.

## Critical Chain

If an executive or manager fails to be an effective sponsor, all individuals reporting to that level and subsequent lower levels will disconnect from the strategy. The higher the level in the organization that experience ineffective sponsorship, the more individuals will disconnect from the strategy. The main reason ineffective sponsorship triggers a disconnect from all the individuals at lower levels is a lack of trust and commitment. Effective sponsorship is not a given, and once it becomes ineffective it allows individuals to disconnect from the strategy. Ineffective sponsorship is a key driver of failed strategy implementations.

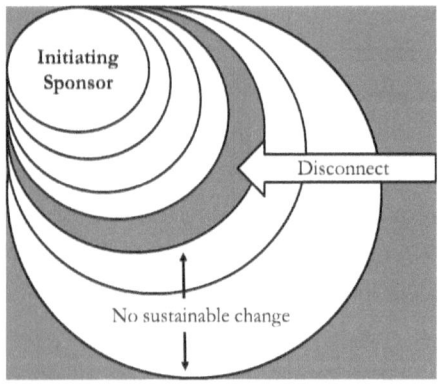

*Figure 2.3. Sponsorship's Critical Chain*

## Sponsorship Development

Leaders are not necessarily managers and managers are not necessarily leaders. Organizations strive to attract high-quality talent with leadership and managerial traits. Organizations recognize the need to have well-balanced leaders in the organization and offer leadership and management skill-development programs.

Sponsorship is a subset of management and focuses on specific services provided to impacted individuals. The general consensus in organizations is that sponsorship is expected, and they don't fully appreciate the role of a sponsor during the implementation of a significant change like a new strategy. This is evident by the fact that sponsorship development programs in organizations are rare.

An example: A small airline company employs thirty-five commercial pilots. The company specializes in flying individuals or small groups to relatively remote areas. They use small four- to ten-passenger planes. All pilots are well-qualified and deliver outstanding service. During their off season, which happens to be the high-risk fire season, the government hired some to fly firefighting missions. What is the probability those well-trained pilots are also skilled in firefighting? To be effective they must get specialized training and an annual refresher course to maintain their firefighting skills.

Executives and managers don't implement significant changes every day. They are focused on running day-to-day operations. Most strategy implementations fail not because of the quality of the strategy but because of the inadequate level of adoption driven by sponsors. Not investing the time and resources in specific sponsorship training is no different than using good pilots to fly firefighting missions. They are set up for failure.

Sponsorship development educates executives and managers on the creation of a change-enabling milieu and the three critical connections. It focuses on determining the quality of the critical connections and how to repair or strengthen these connections when needed. It also provides the opportunity to practice selected elements of effective communication and how to determine their own level of sponsorship. Well-designed sponsorship development programs provide a safe environment for executives to practice their skills and have access to professional executive coaches.

A sponsorship development program will increase the employees' confidence and trust knowing that the strategy implementation will be supported by a cadre of well-educated and developed sponsors. This is an investment worth making.

## *Risk Management*

Effective sponsorship facilitates the development of a strong change-enabling milieu in the organization, one that will facilitate the creation of the three critical connections needed for a successful strategy implementation. Sponsorship is a service and ineffective sponsorship a significant risk to a strategy implementation. Best practices in this field point to the following.

**Be proactive:** Don't make the assumption that all executives and managers will provide effective sponsorship during the implementation of a new strategy. Identify the need for sponsorship development as early in the process as possible. Ensure high-quality skill development and ensure every manager and executive are involved.

**Assess effectiveness:** As stated earlier, the quality of sponsorship is best evaluated by those who are being sponsored. If you want to know if your clients are satisfied with your services, you have to ask. If you want to know how effective the new strategy is sponsored, asked those impacted by the changes. It is of utmost importance that senior executives are fully aware of the level of sponsorship their strategy is receiving because it is the best point in the implementation process to observe a disconnect from the strategy.

**Take action:** When you become aware that a specific executive or manager is not an effective sponsor, take mitigating action. If you do not act quickly *all* those impacted at subsequent levels will disconnect from the strategy. The cost to repair far exceeds the costs associated with early action.

Sponsorship is at the heart of a new strategy development and implementation. Underestimating the significance of the role of the sponsor can and will have significant negative implications for the organization. However, almost all successful strategy implementations are enabled by strong and effective sponsorship.

## Summary

The implementation of a strategy does not occur in a vacuum. Every organization has its own setting with specific elements and dimensions. The significance of the elements varies and is different for every organization. Some of the elements in the milieu appear to be constant over time: culture, history, trust, and expectations, complemented by communication and sponsorship.

The milieus within organizations are not always change enabling. It takes a deliberate effort to adjust the critical elements to create a change-enabling milieu. We have found that each critical element has the ability to derail the implementation of a strategy and should not be overlooked.

Organizations have complex cultures. A strategy implementation does not impact all cultural aspects, but there may be one or two critical aspects that have the potential to derail the implementation. Culture becomes change enabling as soon as the organization identifies and mitigates those aspects that directly impact the implementation. This can be a single belief or a specific set of behaviors.

A high level of trust in the CEO, sponsors, and the strategy as a solution will reduce the cost and time associated with any strategy implementation. The level of trust in the organization can fluctuate significantly from one area to the next. Trust becomes change enabling as soon as the organization identifies the drivers behind the low level of trust and activates effective mitigation actions to increase trust.

Every organization has a history of strategy implementations. This history can enhance or inhibit the implementation of a new strategy. As with the other critical elements, the perceptions about the success or failure of previous implementations can differ vastly within a single organization. It is important to note that it is not only the perception of the senior executives that determine the change enabling ability of this critical element but the perception of all others impacted by the new strategy. The new strategy should clearly be associated or disassociated with past implementations to ensure that this critical element does not negatively impact the present implementation.

A new strategy automatically introduces new expectations. It is vital that organizations have a solid understanding of the new strategy-related expectations. Meeting expectations builds trust and, consequently, become change enabling. It is of utmost importance that organizations manage expectations in order to avoid expectation violation that will cripple the implementation of the strategy.

Communication is the primary tool for distributing key messages in an organization. Individuals need specific, sequential information that can be met through communication during the implementation. A well-coordinated communication plan is a significant asset in any implementation. There are deadly communication mistakes that need to be avoided in order to create a change-enabling milieu: (1) communicating without a clear understanding of the purpose of the messages, (2) communicating without validating the message, (3) communicating through ineffective message-delivery vehicles, (4) communicating without assessing the effectiveness of the communication, (5) communicating only with sponsors (who are not the only communicators in an organization), (6) participating in the confusion trap, and (7) ignoring or failing to identify critical messages.

A change-enabling milieu significantly impacts any strategy implementation. The milieu can hamper and derail the implementation if left unattended. Once it becomes change enabling, it will enhance and expedite the implementation. The most effective approach is to develop a specific plan to enhance and alter every critical element to the point where it becomes change enabling. It is also important to note that *sustaining* the change-enabling milieu is as important as creating it.

The change-enabling milieu is a key ingredient in the creation of the critical connections between the strategy and the impacted individuals. It accelerates the creation of the psychological, structural, and contractual connections. It also assists in sustaining the critical connections and thus significantly contributes to the successful implementation of a new strategy.

The change-enabling milieu is analogous to preparing a swamp in order to build a three-lane highway across it. The swamp can be drained, pylons placed that will serve as the foundation, or filled with rock to stabilize the ground in order to strengthen the road's foundation. Without sufficient preparation, the construction of the road will certainly fail. In preparing the change-enabling milieu, we need to focus on improving trust, communication, sponsorship and managing expectations. A well-developed change-enabling milieu significantly reduces the risk of the critical connections failing and simultaneously increases the sustainability of the connections and strategy.

## Chapter Three

# Psychological Connection

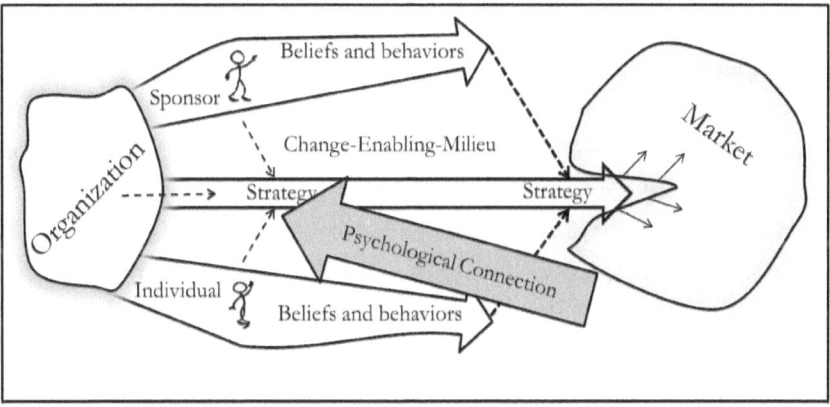

*Figure 3.1. The Psychological Connection in Strategy Implementation*

## The Critical Connections

- *Psychological* connection unlocks individuals' willingness to change their behavior.

- *Structural* connection pinpoints the detailed behavior changes the strategy calls for throughout the organization.

- *Contractual* connection anchors and lock individuals' new negotiated behavior.

# Why Is the Psychological Connection Important?

The simplest way to describe the psychological connection is to compare it to an audience at a Broadway show. The members of the audience are never in a position to do something different or change any behaviors. A change in strategy calls for a change in individual behavior. The psychological connection pulls the individual out of the audience and onto the stage. Once on stage, the individual will engage, assess the situation, and be exposed to the idea of exploring new behaviors. Without a psychological connection, the organization cannot unlock individuals' willingness to change their behavior.

In this context, let's look at other advantages of the psychological connection.

**Creates a safe environment:** The psychological connection creates a relatively safe environment where the individual feels comfortable enough to get engaged in the discussion. A person is highly unlikely to get involved in a new strategy if there is the perception that individuals will be exposed and be vulnerable to "unfair" practices. Establishing the psychological connection ensures that the individual feels safe and protected while engaging in the development and implementation of a new strategy.

**Opens the individual's willingness to question:** It is important to question current practices and look critically at the proposed behavior changes during an implementation. Individuals are encouraged to ask as many questions as needed to make them comfortable enough to change their behavior. The willingness to ask tough questions is advanced by the psychological connection and is important to the change process.

**Stimulates discovery:** As the new strategy calls for new behaviors, it is important that individuals have the opportunity to explore new behaviors and practices that align with the new strategy. Every individual's work environment is slightly different from others', and the ability to discover new avenues that fit the individual's role is vital to the success of the new strategy. The psychological connection simulates this individual discovery process.

**Facilitates personal assessment:** The important question every impacted individual has to ask himself or herself is, "What behavior do I have to change in order to be aligned with the new strategy?" The individual should not question what behavior other people will have to change. It is also of significant importance to the change process that the individual questions his or her personal skills and abilities in the process. If the change in strategy calls for someone to adopt new behaviors that require skills they don't have, resistance to the change will mount and the change will be inhibited. The psychological connection allows individuals to assess personal skills and abilities, believing the organization will provide the support needed to acquire these new skills if needed.

**Promotes experimentation:** A great deal of uncertainty exists when new behaviors are promoted. There is no guarantee that the new processes or behaviors will align with the strategy or that it will deliver the results asked for by the new strategy. Individuals want to be successful and should get the opportunity to experiment with behaviors to see if they will be successful. The psychological connection promotes experimentation allowing the individual to develop trust in the new solution.

**Provides sequential information:** During a change process, individuals prefer receiving change-related information in a specific sequence. The specific sequence allows the individual to systematically deconstruct their current beliefs and behaviors and slowly construct new beliefs and behaviors aligned with the new strategy. This process is critical to the implementation and sustainability of a new strategy. The psychological connection provides the individual with the needed sequential information.

**Guides individuals from unawareness to adoption:** The key to every change is to move all individuals within the organization from unawareness for the need to change to the point where new behaviors are adopted and maintained. The psychological connection connects individuals psychologically to the new strategy and guides them from a point of unawareness to adoption.

The psychological connection pulls the individual "out of the audience and onto the stage" in a safe environment, allowing him or her to discover and practice the new strategy-aligned behaviors. The connection guides the individual from unawareness to adoption. Keeping the connection intact is critical to the success of the strategy. Without the psychological connection, individuals will listen to the CEO when the new strategy is announced, but then they will get up, continuing the work they did yesterday and the day before, tanking the new strategy in the process. Knowing that the psychological connection is important is valuable, but we still need to know how to develop and maintain the connection.

How does an organization develop a psychological connection between the strategy and the individual? Two ingredients are needed to develop the psychological connection. First, develop a change-enabling milieu. Second, communicate specific sequential information to all individuals impacted by the strategy.

The development of the change-enabling milieu is a holistic and integrated approach to change, guided by the following principles.

**Transparency:** The higher the level of transparency in an organization the higher the quality of the connections. It is helpful to create an electronic library where all the information can be made available. Some may argue that all information should not be shared because of its sensitive nature. In my experience, the benefits of transparency far outweigh the risks. We often hear executives say they don't need to put out all the information because the individuals will not read it. It does not matter whether everybody reads all the information. The organization is setting the tone and creating a change-enabling environment in which information sharing and transparency are key.

**Engagement:** People will only become willing to change their behavior if they are engaged and their input is solicited and valued. Their active participation is crucial to establishing all three connections. If people are not engaged, they will not volunteer and will continue with their current behavior despite the behavioral demands of the new strategy.

**Nonpunitive environment:** Individuals have to find and explore new ways to meet the intent of the new strategy. The organization wants the individuals to become psychologically connected to the new strategy. A non-punitive environment promotes the discovery of new procedures and actions. As people get the opportunity to experiment with new behaviors without a fear of retaliation, buy-in is created, as well as a strong personal link to the strategy.

**Support:** Change is hard and most people experience a certain degree of fear and anxiety during a journey of change. They need a safe, change-enabling milieu as well as the support of their primary sponsor.

## Creating the Psychological Connection

Individuals connect psychologically with the strategy as they are moved from a point of unawareness to adoption. This movement is enabled by the organization providing specific and sequential change-related information.

Creating a psychological connection and moving people from unawareness to adoption is two sides of the same coin.

Let's look at this movement through the different identified phases.

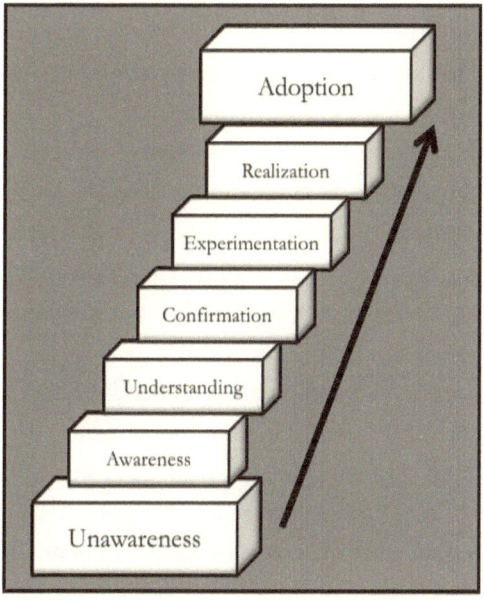

*Figure 3.2. From Unawareness to Adoption*

## *Unawareness*

The eight steps in the change process are the following:

- Unawareness

- Awareness

- Understanding

- Confirmation

- Experimentation

- Realization

- Adoption

The first step in a change process is an impetus to change. As an organization plans a strategy change, organizational members are most likely not aware of the proposed changes. In most organizations, the CEO and the board will be the first to discuss the possibility of a strategy change. As these initial discussions unfold, the opportunity to establish a psychological connection between the strategy and various individuals in the organization arises. At this stage there are only concepts, yet it is the perfect time to start planning the psychological connection. The development of the psychological connection needs to start on day one of the preliminary discussions between the CEO and board members.

The first task of the CEO is to establish a psychological connection between the strategy and the board members. If a CEO is unable to establish the connection, chances are he or she will not be given the opportunity to implement the strategy, and even if given the opportunity, he or she will probably not be successful at establishing the connections at the lower levels either.

How do we develop the psychological connection? Let's look at the flow of information. To start the process, we need to complete a detailed stakeholder analysis. This is done by grouping the members in the organization in functional groups and layers of responsibilities down to the lowest level. The stakeholder analysis is the foundation of the communication plan and regulates the flow of information as the tiers receive the information sequentially.

Let's look at the flow of information and how it develops the psychological connection.

## Awareness

Awareness is more than knowing a change is about to take place. Sending an e-mail to all employees informing them a new strategy is being developed and additional information will be forthcoming is not developing awareness. Specific detailed information needs to be communicated in order to build awareness.

Let's focus on the information an individual needs to become aware of the impact of the new strategy and what constitutes an adequate, appropriate organizational response.

**What information do individuals need?**

The development of awareness pivots on two pieces of information. The first is the case for change and the second is the roadmap. Detailed information is not available at this stage. The following high-level information needs to be communicated.

- What are the results of the current strategy?
- Why is the current state no longer sustainable?
- Why have we not changed earlier?
- What is the alternative?
- How can the organization achieve the alternative?
- What is the high-level transition plan?
- Who, how, where, and when will individuals be engaged in the process?
- How will the strategy development process, business planning process, and the individual change process be integrated?

Most leaders do not see the necessity for communicating this information from the start. They tend to think they don't have sufficient information and employees should only know that they are working on something. Just as a reminder: the failure rate for strategy changes is very high, and there is a reason for this. There is a "golden window" of opportunity that opens at the beginning of the process that enables the organization to develop the psychological connection between the strategy and those impacted. Missing this opportunity leads to significant challenges over time and failure to implement the new strategy.

The dominant questions employees ask during this phase are regarding what is wrong with the current state, what the reason for the new strategy is, what the new strategy potentially offers, and how the organization plans to get to the desired state.

### Organizational response

The organization has two significant opportunities. The first is to develop awareness of the new strategy, and the second is to create the first link in the psychological connection—awareness. The organization must keep these two opportunities in mind as they sequentially create and cascade specific communications to develop awareness. The CEO has to develop a detailed communication containing information about the results of the current strategy, why it is not sustainable, potential alternatives, and a roadmap toward achieving that state.

This communication needs to be complemented by a full set of FAQs. This information is now ready to be shared with the board. They are given the opportunity to engage, raise questions, and poke holes in the information. The information and the FAQs are edited and strengthened. The information is now shared with the senior management group, and they are given the opportunity to engage and refine the information. The communication is now refined to the level where it can be distributed to all managers to discuss with their direct reports. As the information is cascaded throughout the organization it should be accessible to all involved.

The content of the communiqué is structured in the sequence of addressing the why, what, and how questions at a high level, complemented by a visual roadmap. In addition, everybody in the organization is informed of where they can access this information. Well-structured information significantly reduces unofficial information and rumors and reduces confusion.

The purpose of developing awareness is to create the first link of the psychological connection. It is of utmost importance that the organization assesses the level of awareness and the effectiveness of their communication *before* creating the next link, which is the understanding of the new strategy.

There are three significant risks to avoid: (1) inability to develop sponsorship at all management levels; (2) insufficient awareness; and (3) ineffective engagement. These risks can be avoided by building a strong first link in the psychological connection.

Sponsorship for a new strategy implementation is developed by cascading information layer by layer into the organization. It is important to slow down between the layers to solicit and value input and to ensure most of the issues are addressed before the information is shared at the next level. Skipping layers eliminates sponsorship and undermines the communication. Remember, the goal is to develop a psychological connection, and organizations should never underestimate the psychological impact on individuals when sponsors are not engaged in the process.

It is easy to identify insufficient awareness. The conversations in the organization usually reveal the level of awareness. If the issues of the communication are the main points of informal conversation, the need for information has not been addressed sufficiently. As soon as most individuals have adequate information and are fully aware of the developing new strategy, the conversations change to the details of the changes and its potential impact on them. The more people feel engaged in the implementation of a new strategy the stronger the psychological connection between the individuals and the strategy. Cascading the awareness information and the pause to solicit input will enhance the feeling of engagement. When individuals see their input is valued, they become more engaged and develop a strong psychological connection with the strategy.

Once people have sufficient awareness, they tend to seek detailed information about how the change is going to affect them personally. They are ready to move to the understanding phase of the journey.

## Understanding

During this phase, the dominant question becomes "how." Individuals get a sense that the new strategy is calling for changes that will impact them and that they need detailed information.

### What information do individuals need?

Individuals need specific details about how the strategy will impact their day-to-day activities. This information is not available at this time. The value of the psychological connection becomes evident in the individual's willingness to discover the details of the impact collaboratively with their sponsors.

### Organizational response

At this stage, the sponsors facilitate the process of discovery that will flush out the details of the strategy. Executives never develop a strategy to the smallest level of detail before they roll it out. They develop the framework and let the impacted individuals fill in the blanks. The organization uses the strategy to point the direction and facilitate the discovery of the details at the individual level. Individuals are allowed to identify the changes they will have to make to align with the new strategy. As individuals in similar positions with similar challenges share this information, the change process is accelerated. Best practices are shared, and people are encouraged when they learn that they are not the only ones affected. Individuals get the opportunity to be creative and solve the problems the new strategy might pose. Sharing information also creates the second link of the psychological connection.

Organizations can use custom portals, electronic workspaces, or collaborative social media sites to allow individuals to share the detailed information. The organization needs to be prepared for the deluge of information. A well-organized electronic workspace will serve the purpose.

As the details are discovered at the individual level, an important reconciliation takes place. Individuals reconcile their understanding of the changes needed with their current day-to-day practices. It is the organization's responsibility to verify that the collaborative details are aligned with the strategy and that they hold the potential to deliver the expected results. We call it the first round of reconciliation. Will all the proposed changes at the individual level roll up to the intended outcome the strategy calls for? The role of the supporting sponsors at all levels are critical to the verification process seeing that they have to become fully aware of all the details, and make a professional judgment whether the changes have the potential to deliver the intended results.

There are two significant risks to avoid: (1) working in silos, and (2) weakening sponsorship.

Individuals in the organization seek solutions and alternatives that will bring the new strategy to fruition. A danger is that if people with similar challenges are working in silos, different solutions are developed for the same challenges. Once people develop their own solutions, they become defensive and turf oriented. A divided team effort does not effectively promote the strategy.

During this phase, all supporting sponsors listen to what their direct reports are willing to commit to in order to make the strategy work. Supporting sponsors have the time to engage with the details and let the subordinates know which changes are acceptable and will be sponsored and which will not.

The creation of the second link in the psychological connection is the focus of this phase. The connection is not only between the individuals and the strategy but between the individuals, their sponsors, and the strategy. It is of utmost importance that the supporting sponsors are fully engaged and that the organization strengthens their sponsorship through the discovery of the detailed changes.

If the individuals clarified the new changes and developed a high level of understanding of the changes and its potential implications, the second link in the psychological connection has been forged. In the next step, individuals look to their supporting sponsors to confirm their sponsorship.

## *Confirmation*

All individuals are now fully aware of the new strategy and have a detailed appreciation about how they would need to change their day-to-day behavior to realize the strategy's intended results.

They now turn to their sponsors and inquire whether they will be sponsored and supported in making the changes.

### What Information do Individuals Need?

Individuals want to hear, see, and experience that the leaders at all levels are on the same page and will support all the changes needed to bring the strategy to fruition. Change is difficult, and they want to know that they will be supported to the end. Individuals will "test" their sponsor's strength of sponsorship because they want to be confident that the support will be available to them when the road gets more challenging. They want to be confident that the sponsors will be with them for the full duration of the implementation and not abandon them down the road.

How does the organization respond to the individual's need for sponsorship-related information?

### Organizational response

The organization should define, describe, and clarify the role of the supporting sponsors at all levels. The information about the sponsor's role should be communicated to everybody in the organization. Some organizations choose to strengthen the sponsorship through workshops. It builds trust if this information is shared. Defining the role of the sponsor and sharing it publicly builds trust in sponsors and is needed to create the third link, confirming sound sponsorship, of the psychological connection.

An important aspect of the organizational response at this time is to link every impacted individual to one specific supporting sponsor who will provide the individual with the support and services needed to make the necessary changes. Linking individuals to sponsors reduces confusion and strengthens the psychological connection during this phase.

Verify that each impacted individual is well-connected to his or her sponsor. The verification process will identify individuals who may be trapped in matrix relationships and not directly linked to a specific sponsor. This initial stakeholder analysis should be used for this purpose.

There are two significant risks to avoid during this process. The first is matrix relationships. In a matrix relationship an individual will have more than one person he or she reports to. Multiple reporting relationships add significant complexity to effective sponsorship. The second is a broken chain of supporting sponsors. When a manager is not acting as an effective sponsor, it inhibits all individuals reporting to him and his direct reports in going through the change process effectively.

Individuals reporting to more than one sponsor run the risk of psychologically disconnecting from the strategy. They don't really know which direction to go and they select a default direction where they experience the least pain without truly buying into the solution. Once people in matrix relationships have been identified, the organizational structure may be adjusted for an interim period to align with the strategy.

Every supporting sponsor should be linked to another sponsor who can function as a backup. Wherever the critical sponsor chain is detached, the psychological connection will not be leaving those individuals in the dark with all its consequences.

## Experimentation

As individuals move from unawareness to adopting new behaviors, they identify with new practices or procedures. They need a high level of confidence that the new behaviors will generate the intended results before they wholeheartedly adopt it. They need to experiment with the behaviors. This can be done during a pilot implementation, where lessons learned can be shared throughout the organization and will thus improve the quality of the overall change. Without the opportunity to experiment, individuals will hesitate to embrace the change and may abandon it altogether when unexpected results surface.

**What information do individuals need?**

Sharing the results of the experimentation is critical during the experimental phase and should include the following information: (1) a detailed description of the experiment; (2) results; (3) lessons learned; and (4) generalization of the results. Sharing this information company wide with a high level of transparency will help move the individuals through this phase of the journey.

The individuals want to have confidence that the changes or new practices are working before they abandon their current behavior and embrace the new. All the information that will build trust and confidence should be shared as the data becomes available.

**Organizational response**

It is valuable to share the experimentation results as it builds confidence in the solutions.

It is not only the sharing of results that is important at this time. The organization needs to identify opportunities to acknowledge and reward individuals who have embraced the new strategy, developed aligned behaviors, and participated in a successful experiment. The structure of the communications will have a dual purpose—announcing results and lessons learned on one hand, and acknowledging progress and individuals on the other.

The organization has to verify that all the experiments, results, and lessons learned were received by everybody in the organization. The experimental phase intends to demonstrate that the developed strategy has the potential to deliver the intended results. The demonstration instills confidence in everyone who is responsible for making the strategy work. Positive results at this time enhance the trust in the strategy and in the individual's ability to adjust and deliver.

There are two significant risks to avoid: inadequate experimentation, and not incorporating the lessons learned into the full implementation. Sometimes organizations make the mistake of deciding that experimentation is not worth the investment. This is a fallacy, because if experimentation does not occur, the first full implementation of the strategy is actually an organization-wide experiment. The organization is then conducting a full experiment without acknowledging it. Most of the time the psychological connection becomes disconnected because "unproven" practices are implemented without them having been tested. A few experiments with high-risk practices will be sufficient to create this link of the psychological connection.

Experiments usually surface weaknesses in the new behaviors or procedures. Lessons from the experimentation need to be incorporated into the full implementation of the strategy. Overlooking this will be frustrating and may have a demoralizing effect as well as weaken the psychological connection.

At this point, the psychological connection is now fully developed and intact. The organization is ready for a full implementation of the strategy. The individuals were moved from a point of unawareness to the point where the strategy can be deployed in the organization. Once the strategy is fully implemented, the organization needs to let it run and assess to what degree the strategy will realize the intended results.

## Realization

Realizing the intended results is the last but most critical step on the journey from unawareness to adoption. The realization ultimately determines whether the strategy will be adopted or not. Even if every aspect of the development and implementation of the new strategy went smoothly, if the results are poor the associated changes will not be sustainable and individuals will revert back to the way they did things before, sinking the new strategy.

**What information do individuals need?**

Individuals need information related to progress and success. Every person is now fully involved in the new strategy and executing to the best of their ability while waiting on the results.

**Organizational response**

The organization's response to the individual's need for realization information is limited to time sensitive results (e.g., monthlies and/or quarterlies, as well as success stories). Constant reminders of true results and success stories maintain the psychological connection and increase individuals' willingness to stay on track.

Realization information needs to be distributed throughout the organization. The results should be available to all members. It is the individual incremental contribution to the strategy that fuels the sustainability of the changes and keeps the psychological connection strong.

At this stage, messages should consist of a healthy mix of results and success stories. Organizations have leveraged social media with great success in the past, and they are encouraged to find new and creative ways to share progress and success.

As more individuals are made fully aware of the improved results due to the strategy change, the higher the probability that full adoption will occur.

As more people are recognized and rewarded for their work, the more likely the adoption.

Any change in strategy takes time to work through the organization and market. One of the danger points is the strategy not delivering the expected results, regardless of a full and successful implementation. The risk is that the individuals will realize that the strategy is not working and the organization will experience a disconnect between the strategy and the impacted individuals. The organization should monitor the progress carefully and develop significant mitigation strategies as alternatives to maintain the connection and the intended results. An effective mitigation strategy is to provide the results achieved by the strategy to all impacted individuals. The constant flow of results information will minimize a disconnect at this stage of the change.

When a changing environment negatively impacts the results, the organization needs to protect the strategy by informing everybody why there was a negative impact, the scope of the impact, and the potential influence on the final results *before* the the results are visible. Proactive mitigation will not only protect the psychological connection but strengthen it. Any reactions or comments after the fact may sound like an excuse and could cause significant damage to the strategy.

## Adoption

Adoption is a logical consequence of the realization of the intended results and the creation of the psychological connection between those impacted and the strategy.

The adoption of new and aligned behavior is associated with progress. What started off as the new strategy and the desired state has now become the current state and the current strategy. The change can be viewed as sustainable, and the stage is set for a new round of strategy changes.

The psychological connection established during the process will stay in place with all the members who participated in the process. Anybody joining the organization after the fact will not have a psychological connection to the strategy. This is a significant and important observation for two reasons. First, if an organization has a 10 percent staff turnover rate, the strategy will weaken over time as new members join the organization seeing that they are not connected to the strategy. This risk can be mitigated through a well-designed on-boarding process. Second, the longer people work within the framework of a strategy they have helped develop, the stronger the psychological connection becomes and the harder it is to disconnect them when a new change is needed.

## Strength of the Psychological Connection

In the beginning of this chapter, we described the psychological connection between the new strategy and those impacted. We want individuals aware of the strategy and engaged to such an extent that they are enabled to make the necessary changes. Questions that often surface are concerning how strong the connection is and how fundable it is.

The strength of the psychological connection is influenced by the organization's response to the individual's need for information to change and how carefully and deliberately they were moved from unawareness to adoption. When an organization pays sufficient attention to detail, a stronger connection can be developed. The faster an organization rushed to get it done, the more brittle the connection.

## Identifying a Weak Psychological Connection

Organizations have several opportunities to assess the quality of the psychological connection during an implementation. The first opportunity arises after the awareness phase, when an assessment should be done to measure the quality of the connection.

What does the assessment consist of, and how much time and resources will it take to complete? The assessment can be done through a simple personal interview process involving a small sample size. In addition, monitoring the interaction between individuals during the engagement process will signal the quality of the connection. The feedback loop will provide the last segment of the assessment. The amount of feedback on the FAQs will slow down, signaling that it is time to move to the next step.

Sponsorship assessments can be done at any time, as often as needed, to identify weaknesses. It is crucial that organizations have a deliberate plan to assess sponsorship frequently, seeing that a weakening in sponsorship can occur at any level, at anytime, anywhere in the organization. This will paralyze all individuals reporting to the weak sponsor. The higher the organization level the sponsor is, the bigger the impact he or she will have on the strategy. Identifying weak sponsorship early is paramount to maintaining a sound psychological connection in the organization.

## Indications of a Weakening Connection

There are signs of a weakening connection organizations can pick up on. Conversations will revert back to issues that were prominent in the awareness phase. Individuals will start questioning the original drivers of the change or elements in the original business case. This delayed reaction is symptomatic of a weakening psychological connection. The deterioration of the connection poses a significant risk to the new strategy and can potentially kill it.

Declining sponsorship signals danger to the new strategy. As the psychological connection weakens, so will the sponsorship support of those impacted. Individuals will slowly pull back from the new strategy and move into a holding pattern, where they will observe the changes in sponsorship. If they experience weakening sponsorship, they will disconnect from the psychological connection—with devastating consequences to the strategy. Sponsorship weakening can occur any time and any place in the organization and it will spread like wildfire if not mitigated.

Another problem occurs when executives deviate from the answers they provided in the FAQs. Developing the FAQs enabled the executives to stay unified and lead the change in strategy. As time passed and the executives became inundated with issues, they started deviating from their original position without coordinating amongst themselves. This deviation signaled a weakening of sponsorship from the top and opened the door for most individuals to hunker down and wait. They observed the rift, and if not addressed, people disconnect from the strategy and label the effort as just another "fly-by-night" exercise. The likelihood that the organization will be able to reenergize the strategy and regain momentum at this point is slim.

Limited experimentation may trigger individuals to slow down and wait. They are uncertain and don't want to commit to a strategy while wondering whether the newly designed solutions will deliver results. The more the organization pushes the new solutions without adequate experimentation, the more likely the individuals will distance themselves from the new strategy, resulting in a potential psychological disconnect.

## Repairing a Weak Psychological Connection

How does the organization repair a weak or broken psychological connection to the point the new strategy is not at risk?

The first step is to immediately identify the problem. The longer the weakening continues, the more difficult it becomes to repair. Repairing a weakening connection becomes more challenging as time passes because more individuals are involved. If the problem is unattended until disconnected by the critical mass, reconnecting it becomes nearly impossible. One additional aspect to keep in mind is that the more individuals involved and the weaker the connection, the more resources will be needed to repair the damage.

The second point is to know what is driving the weakening in the psychological connection. The key is to identify the symptoms early, understand the root cause, and develop a mitigation plan. It is not possible to describe all the potential drivers that can weaken the connection. If sponsorship is the driver, it needs to be the focus of the recovery plan.

The biggest risk for organizations is that they have not deployed mechanisms to identify the drivers behind a weakening connection in advance. They are unable to get to the problem fast enough to stop it, resulting in a psychological disconnect with significant negative impact to the new strategy. Developing and implementing tools that monitor the situation from beginning to end is critical to overcoming this problem.

## Summary

The psychological connection unlocks individuals' willingness to change their behavior. Without this willingness, strategy implementations cannot succeed. It is of utmost importance that organizations focus on the development of a sound psychological connection between the strategy and all impacted individuals.

Creating this connection originates with a sound understanding of the current beliefs in the organization as well as how those beliefs drive current behaviors and potential opposing beliefs. Opposing beliefs need to be identified, verified, and made visible in order to change them into beliefs that will support the new strategy.

Impacted individuals who travel on a well-designed journey will go from unawareness to adopting the new strategy-aligned behaviors. This journey is not possible without meeting the individuals' strategy-related information needs. Organizations have a responsibility to provide individuals with the specific sequential information they need to change. If the psychological connection is not forged, individuals might make a few changes, but those changes will not be sustained. This will have a significant impact on the success of the strategy as it requires a stable and sustainable change in behavior.

Maintaining a sound psychological connection is paramount to the implementation of the strategy. It not only serves the individual with incremental information but is intertwined with the other connections. The other connections cannot be effective without the psychological connection.

## CHAPTER FOUR

# Structural Connection

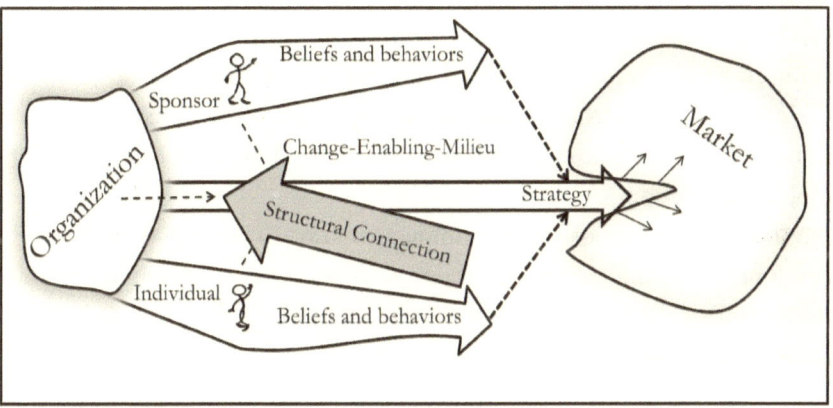

*Figure 4.1. The Structural Connection in Strategy Implementation*

## The Critical Connections

- *Psychological* connection unlocks individuals' willingness to change their behavior.

- *Structural* connection pinpoints the detailed behavior changes the strategy calls for throughout the organization.

- *Contractual* connection anchors and lock individuals' new negotiated behavior.

# Why Is a Structural Connection Important?

A new strategy begins as a concept in an executive's mind. The concept slowly gathers momentum as people figure out whether it is practical. The ideas and concepts of the strategy are thought-provoking but eventually demand a functional approach to make it a reality.

We have stressed the importance of creating a psychological connection, which unlocks individuals' willingness to become personally involved in the success of the new strategy by changing their behavior. The willingness needs to link to the intended results.

The structural connection is developed to translate the strategy into the organization's business plans. The strategy is translated into strategic drivers and broken into action steps at the individual level. There should be a clear, visible link between the strategy and the day-to-day operations reflected in the business plan.

In this chapter, we will focus on the importance of the structural connection and how it is developed and maintained to significantly increase the odds of a successful strategy implementation. We will explore ways to test the strength of the structural connection and how to mitigate a weak or broken connection.

The failure rate of strategy implementation is alarming, and a well-developed structural connection is one of three crucial connections necessary to implement a strategy successfully; the other being the psychological and contractual connections.

## *The Structural Connection Enables the Transfer of the Strategy to the Individual Level (Cascading)*

The new strategy is first developed at a macro level. It expresses the general direction at a global, national, and state level. For example, AAV Pharmaceuticals developed a goal to increase their revenue to four billion dollars over the next three years and market share 15 percent. This expression of the strategy is so general that individuals in the organization cannot really connect with it. Tom Black, the sales representative in the local Phoenix office of AAV Pharmaceuticals does not really comprehend what the new strategy has to do with him. The structural connection transfers the macro strategy to the local and individual level. The connection facilitates the process of transforming the strategy into action steps for Tom Black. It enables Tom to visualize himself in the new strategy and provides the details for how he can support the strategy. The connection makes the strategy meaningfully at the individual level.

Evidence that a structural connection between the strategy and business plans has been created can be found in key organizational documents. A good structural connection is evident when the key strategic drivers are embedded in the organization's business plans. If the structural connection has not been made, the operations of the organization point in a different direction than the strategy.

## The Structural Connection Translates the Strategy into Individual Action Steps (Key Strategy Drivers)

A change in strategy calls for a change in the day-to-day activities and behaviors of individuals throughout the organization. The structural connection translates the strategy to specific aligned-action steps. This translation is fundamental to the success of the strategy and is the critical link between the psychological, structural, and administrative connections. At some point every impacted individual will ask, "What do I need to do differently to make the new strategy work?" This connection provides the answer.

A documentation review will determine if and to what extent the organization has transferred the strategy into functional action steps, scaled to the applicable level, and refined to measurable units.

## The Structural Connection Cascades the Success Metrics throughout the Organization

We all struggle to define success metrics that are meaningful and valuable in a decision-making process. When AAV Pharmaceuticals declared they wanted to increase their revenue to $4B (an annual increase of $400M), they knew that every local office would need to contribute to make it happen. The structural connection allows the systematic cascading of the overarching strategy goals down to the individual level. It also enables the reconciliation of the success metric from the lowest level to the highest. For example, if

Tom Black (the sales rep in the local Phoenix office) can only commit to 80 percent of the revenue increase the strategy calls for, the goals will not be met. The upward reconciliation of all ground-floor commitments triggers an adjustment of the goals to make it feasible.

## The Structural Connection Aligns the Strategy and Business Plans

An old business axiom suggests a variety of ways to accomplish something: (1) doing the wrong things right; (2) doing the right things wrong; (3) doing the wrong things wrong; and (4) doing the right things right. The structural connection aligns the new strategy with the new business plans, enabling the individuals to do the right things the right way, enhancing the strategy. Scrutinizing current business plans may reveal the potential misalignment with the current strategy.

## Creating the Structural Connection

Most business plans reflect operational actions that are fundamental in keeping the doors open. The direct link between the strategy and individual actions is often absent. This phenomenon is even more evident at the lower levels of the organization.

Organizations clearly struggle to link the strategy to simple action steps at the individual level with significant consequences. The strategy calls for a movement in one direction, and if individuals are moving in a different direction, it will not be long before this tension leads to a correction, and in 63 percent of the cases the strategy gives way (Mankins & Steele, January 2006). That begs the questions of how the structural connection can be helpful in this process and how it can be created.

Individuals have limited adaptation capacity (Conner, 2006). They can only endure so much change before they show signs of overload that will hamper the development and implementation of any additional changes. The structural connection is created through the existing business planning process, which people are already familiar and comfortable with.

The existing business-planning process reflects the day-to-day operations as well as special investments that are project driven. The framework of the structural connection is developed from the current business-planning process.

The psychological, structural, and administrative connections are synchronized so all connections share the same timeslot. We call it a "gate." Most processes allow the organization to synchronize time frames and insert a gate in the process. The gate is a slight change in the business-planning process, where the owners of the sub-business plans have to present them to senior leadership, demonstrating how their plans align with the new strategy. They also declare the level of support needed to achieve the strategic goals and matrix. The gate is a critical success element because it creates the opportunity where senior leadership can discover how the strategy was translated, transferred, and aligned with the day-to-day operation of the organization.

The first step in the creation of the structural connection is the synchronization of several processes and the introduction of a gate control in the business-planning process.

The next step is the separation of the day-to-day activities and the strategic goals in the business plans.

## *Strategy Compared to Day-to-Day Operations*

One of the current weaknesses in business plans, if we generalize, is the barely observable separation between the day-to-day operational activities and those linked to the strategy. A structural connection becomes strong and effective when there is a clear separation in the business plans between operational activities and strategy-related actions.

A new strategy comes to life when the business plan points to the operational activities with its associated budget and those activities that bring the strategy to fruition and its associated budget. This visual separation in the business plan develops awareness about how much time and resources are committed to keeping the doors open versus promoting the strategy. It is safe to loosely apply the 20/80 rule, with 20 percent of the plan focused on activities that are keeping the doors open and 80 percent focused on moving the strategy forward. This is not a fixed ratio, but organizations whose business plans and resources focus extensively on the strategy are more likely to realize their intended results. As stated before, not realizing the intended results will weaken or disconnect the individuals from the strategy and send it on a road to failure.

The structural connection is created through a relatively small but significant change to the business-planning process by inserting a gate function and separating day-to-day activities and strategic actions in the documented business plan. Creating the structural connection is one side of the challenge. The other side is how the organization cascades the strategy through the process.

## *Cascading the Strategy through the Structural Connection*

Early on the strategy is conceptually developed and vaguely explained at a high level. The content and format are not meaningful at the individual level. For the strategy to get traction, it needs to be translated into practical action steps that can be executed at the individual level. Leveraging the qualities of the structural connection allows the organization to translate the strategy and transfer it from one level to the impacted individual. Let's look briefly at key elements in the process.

The first step is identifying the key drivers of the strategy, the five or six action items that will bring the strategy to life.

For example, AAV Pharmaceuticals's new corporate strategy is to focus their business efforts to (1) gain access to large retail stores; (2) become the primary provider of medications in the western region of the United States; and (3) focus their marketing on over-the-counter medications over the next five years. It is predicted that this strategy will increase their revenue by $400M, a clear and compelling strategy for the organization.

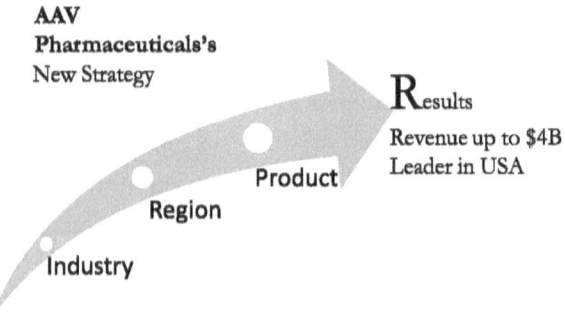

*Figure 4.2. AAV Pharmaceuticals's Corporate Strategy*

Although the strategy is clear and focused, it still does not mean much to the regional manager in Arizona, the office manager in Phoenix, and Tom Black, the sales rep in the Phoenix office. A critical step is to distill the strategy to the five or six steps that will realize the strategy at the individual level. These are called the strategic drivers. Individuals will develop action steps aligned with the strategic drivers.

# Alignment

AAV Pharmaceuticals identified six strategic drivers that, if executed well throughout the organization, will result in the increase of their revenue to four billion dollars within three years after the implementation of the strategy. AAV's executives believe that if each individual takes their lead from these six drivers, the strategy will be successful.

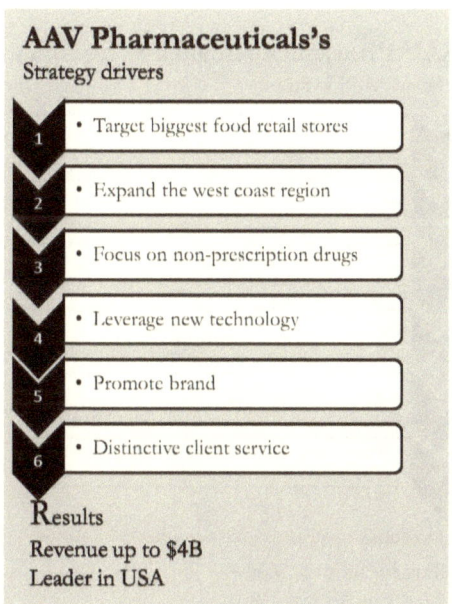

*Figure 4.3. AAV Pharmaceuticals's Strategy Drivers*

The structural connection will enable the organization to cascade the strategy to the lowest levels in the organization. Each level will start with the strategic drivers and then develop appropriate actions for that specific level. This action promotes the alignment process.

Cindy Smith, the manager at the Phoenix local office, who is the sponsor of the change in the office, was given the opportunity to interpret, translate, and select the best action steps that not only align with the strategic drivers but will also make a positive contribution to the expected revenue growth. These action steps are only applicable to the local Phoenix office, developed by the local team. The local office team developed a high level of confidence that the action steps are practical and achievable, and the expected results are within reach of the office. They also reached the conclusion that they can increase their revenue to $250M, which will be their committed contribution toward the strategy and executive team goals.

As the Phoenix office developed their plan, Tom Black asked how he could make a committed contribution to the strategy.

Tom sat with the office manager and identified the six actions he personally had to commit to in order for him to help the office realize its goals and indirectly enable AAV to achieve their goals.

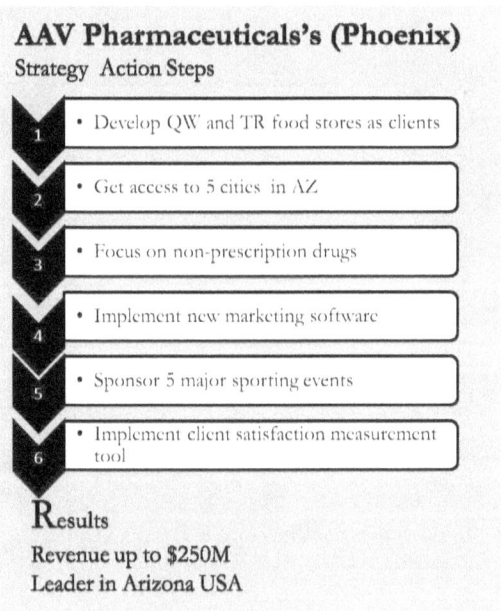

**AAV Pharmaceuticals's (Phoenix)**
Strategy Action Steps

1. • Develop QW and TR food stores as clients
2. • Get access to 5 cities in AZ
3. • Focus on non-prescription drugs
4. • Implement new marketing software
5. • Sponsor 5 major sporting events
6. • Implement client satisfaction measurement tool

**R**esults
Revenue up to $250M
Leader in Arizona USA

*Figure 4.4. Strategy Action Steps of the Phoenix Office of AAV Pharmaceuticals*

Tom is satisfied because he can see how the work he is planning is directly linked to the new strategy. He is also fully aware of what his peers will be doing and that every individual's contribution is valued and important in the process.

There is also another aspect that may surface at this time. Tom and his sponsor may discover that he needs to develop a specific skill or needs additional training in an area in order for him to be successful in the new strategy implementation. An aggregate of all the needs will flow into the development of a training support plan if needed.

The structural connection is thus created and the intent of the strategy cascaded to all levels in the organization.

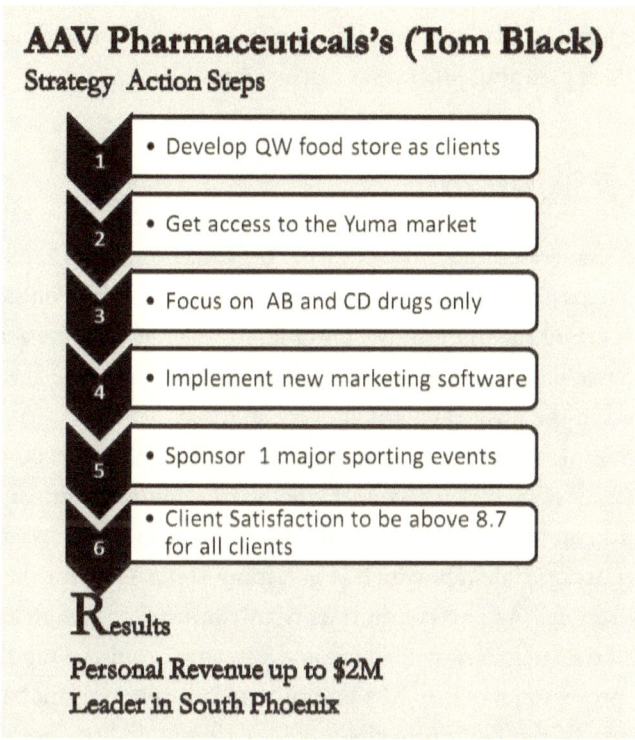

*Figure 4.5. Individual Action Steps*

## Syndication

The key strategic drivers are not arbitrarily selected. Individual engagement is not only important in the creation of the psychological connection but during the process of creating the structural connection. The interaction between every level in the organization is critical to the strength of the structural connection. The syndication not only strengthens the connection between the coworkers but between individuals and their supervisors. The syndication process takes place between every level and is enacted at the next level once agreement regarding the action steps has been reached. This sounds like a slow and never-ending process but when done well, it only takes a few days, with significant gains in the quality of the structural connection.

The syndication and cascading processes culminate in the development of business plans at all levels. The big question is, "What level of investment of resources will 'Tom Black' need to be successful when executing his action plan commitments?" Insight into this question comes from the gate created in the business planning process, as discussed earlier.

## Validation of Business Plans

As the strategy cascades down in the organization, every level develops the actions steps needed to move the strategy forward. The action steps of the higher level create the input to the lower level. It is not only the action steps that cascade down but the performance/success metric as well. These actions are captured in the business plans at every level.

A degree of uncertainty develops among the senior executives as the strategy cascades down. They wonder whether the commitments at the lower levels will add up to the organizational goal. It is this level of uncertainty that drives the next crucial step, which is obtaining feedback from the different levels and reconciling the commitments to confirm. Although the action plans and the strategy are syndicated and cascaded from the top down, the validation process moves from the bottom up. This is important because the reconciliation of the commitments provides a more realistic picture of the potential results of the strategy. The new strategy's traction can be measured against the level of commitment to deliver on the action items at the individual level.

## Reconciliation

Cascading the new strategy from the top down is vital to creating the structural connection. However, it is the return commitments that provide a more accurate prediction of the potential results. We have often observed that an organization sets a financial goal (e.g., improve revenue to $200M in the next fiscal year), but utterly fails to deliver. Organizations will take this set goal, allocate expected growth goals, and assume it will automatically realize the goal over the allocated timeframe. This is far from the truth.

Reconciliation is one of the most reliable ways to predict the results a strategy may yield. In addition, the organization will engage all the impacted individuals and let them determine not only what is possible, but more importantly, what goals they are confident to achieve and are willing to be held accountable for.

The commitment to achieve a specific result is the starting point for the upward reconciliation. If the individuals self-select a commitment (e.g., to change practices that will increase his or her revenue by $500k), and the probability of his or her success is 80 percent, the true value of the commitment that roll up to corporate level is only $400k. The reconciliation of all the commitments from the ground level up to the corporate level usually results in a more realistic growth goal for the organization. If the reconciliation is complete and adds up to only $180M, the executives then have the option to accept this and drive the strategy or make changes to the strategy that may yield higher results. Either way, the reconciliation aspect of the cascading process is fundamental to the success of the strategy.

## Contracting

Another common organizational occurrence is that an individual is charged with increasing revenue, and although there is verbal commitment, at the end of the allocated time frame there is no real revenue increase. At the same time, the individual receives an outstanding performance review and bonus. How is this possible? Contracting is the missing element in the equation. When individuals are charged with the challenge to increase revenue, and they actively engage in working out the details of the changes, receiving effective sponsorship, they should commit to achieving the goal. In addition to the commitment, they should agree on the consequences, positive or negative, of their performance. If the goal is not achieved there has to be consequences.

The lack of fundamental accountability is more often than not the Achilles' heel of a strategy. Organizations struggle to pin down accountability due to their internal culture and history. The cascading process is not only critical to the creation of the structural connection, it is the foundation of accountability.

## Define Success Metrics

The performance of a strategy should be measured from different perspectives to overcome the embedded deficiencies inherent in most measurements. AAV Pharmaceuticals wants to increase revenue by 5 percent or $400M and gain market share of 15 percent over the next three years. AAV will increase revenue without gaining market share if the overall economy grows at 5 percent as well. Was the revenue growth due to the strategy or the economy? We often see hedge fund goals expressed as 3 percent higher than the S&P performance for the year. They set a goal to outperform another known entity.

Most organizations struggle to define success metrics that reflect the impact of the strategy only. So many variables come into play that the leadership team gets discouraged trying to define success in exact terms. The more global the measurement the easier it is to define it.

The challenge organizations face is that a change in strategy calls for a change in behavior at the individual level, but if the performance at the individual level cannot be measured, the organization will not be able to get individual commitments or accountability.

It is relatively easy to define a success metric at a global level. Let's take revenue as an example: the vast majority of people in an organization may not be directly involved in direct revenue generation. For example, many people are involved in designing and building a vehicle at a manufacturing plant. Although they are all contributing to the revenue, their individual actions are not that easily tied to the revenue of the sold vehicle.

A second challenge in defining success metrics at the individual level is not only is it complex, it is time-consuming. This complexity hampers organizations in drilling the strategy to the individual level. These challenges, although daunting, can be solved. Continued hesitation to follow these steps hampers strategy implementation and sustainability.

The most effective approach in designing success metrics at the individual level is tying the success metric creation process to the cascading process. As an organization cascades the action steps that support the strategy from one level to another it needs to identify the appropriate metric along with it. A rule of thumb is, if an action step is not measurable, the individual will get disconnected from the strategy. The higher the number of individuals who disconnect the weaker the strength of the structural connection will become over time. A deteriorating connection will eventually lead to the failure of the strategy. It is thus important to measure as many action steps as possible at the individual level.

In the case of AAV Pharmaceuticals, sales rep Tom Black must have a clear understanding that his small contribution is the foundation of the company's success, and it should be measurable and measured. Tom must be part of the discussion to define his new strategy-aligned action steps and commit to them.

The identification of the success metric at all levels is fundamental to the success of the strategy.

## Monitoring

The structural connection enables an organization to develop clearly defined action steps and cascade them throughout the organization. The connection also lets the organization establish well-defined success measures down to the lowest level. The strategy will unfold over time, and this makes monitoring the progress extremely important and allows us to bring the new strategy implementation to a different level. Monitoring the strategy and this connection will focus on (1) sustainability of the action steps; (2) movement toward the set goals; (3) sponsorship; and (4) recontracting and adjustments.

One of the focus areas to monitor is the selected actions steps, which represent the change in behavior needed to realize the new strategy. A normal trend is to select the new action steps and have people adhere to them for a while, but as they find them challenging they slowly revert back to the old ways, undoing the new strategy. Reverting back to old ways and abandoning the new action steps is symptomatic of a deteriorating connection and should be identified as soon as possible.

Most set goals will be achieved over relatively long periods of time. Revenue growth is not increasing because of the implementation of the new strategy but by the changed behavior over time. It is important for an organization to monitor the progress toward the individual goals over time to determine if and how the organization is making progress toward the overarching goals. This level of monitoring enables the organization to be fully aware of areas where higher or lower than expected growth occurred; making it easier to design mitigation actions as needed.

It was previously stated that a new strategy calls for a change in behavior and that sponsorship is critical to the success of the change. The individual will be changing behaviors and practices and depends on his or her sponsor for continuous support. Declining sponsorship becomes evident when individuals slowly revert back to old practices and the supporting sponsor does not take corrective action. The supporting sponsor may be focusing on other challenges for the moment and unintentionally lets people abandon the new strategy. It is important that the organization monitors sponsorship effectiveness as it is paramount for sustainability.

The selection of a new strategy is not a guarantee that every individual will reach his selected goals with ease. As reality sets in, and individuals implement behavioral changes to act on the new strategy, they may encounter unforeseen realities. Should they change their behavior accordingly and the results of their actions do not yield the expected results, the organization should adjust the action steps or the expected goals for the particular individual. An organization may adjust the selected action steps or only the goals. Every time there is an adjustment of the goals at the individual level it impacts the overarching goal. It is important, therefore, that the organization monitors individuals' performance in regular intervals. This will allow the organization to adjust the expectations as the strategy unfolds and predict organizational performance more accurately.

## Strength of the Structural Connection

The stronger the structural connection, the higher the probability the strategy implementation will be successful and yield the expected results. The structural connection identifies the details to which the impacted individuals will have to commit. The strength of the structural connection is reflected in the level of details and the specificity of the agreed behavioral changes. The more clarity about what the impacted individuals have to change, the stronger the structural connection.

A structural connection expedites the development of the contractual connection. The contractual connection will incorporate all the changes identified during the development of the structural connection. The smoother the transition between these two connections, the stronger the structural connection.

Creating structural connection surfaces two major questions. First, how does an organization know that the structural connection was fully developed? Second, how does an organization identify a deteriorating connection and repair it in time to prevent the strategy from failing?

The quality and strength of the structural connection are evident in two areas: by the paper trails between the strategy, business plans, and the individual's goals; and by the link to the contractual connection. These will be discussed in detail in the next chapter. By reviewing these links, the structural connection and quality of this connection can be determined.

AAV Pharmaceuticals conducted a review of the structural connection prior to developing the new strategy. They looked at the business plans at all levels and the strategy at the time. They interviewed the executives who were confident there was a direct link between the old strategy and their direct reports. The results were surprising. The documentation revealed that there was no connection between the old strategy, the business plans, and the impacted individuals.

## *Identifying a Deteriorating or Broken Structural Connection*

Organizations will not be able to identify and repair any structural connection if they don't develop and implement a plan to monitor the structural connection. The identification process consists of two monitoring practices. The first is a single data-collection event (a snapshot), the second a continuous data-collection process.

The single data-collection event is an internal review of the paper trail between the strategy and all impacted individuals. A small internal review team can perform this task in a few days with a high level of accuracy. The team will review the strategy, business plans, and how the plans cascade down to the different levels of the impacted individuals. They will also look at the reconciliation action and how that action impacted the overarching goals. The document review should uncover areas in the organization where the connection was not well developed and is therefore weak. The findings of the internal review team are important to the discovery of the weak links and will be the first line of repair or mitigation.

Continuous monitoring focuses on the following:

Are regular reviews performed where all individuals are examined from the lowest to the highest level in the organization? This is an interactive process where the results from the top are reconciled with the performance at the individual level. There is a fundamental mistake executives can make. Let's say AAV Pharmaceuticals's new strategy calls for an increase in revenue of $400m over four years, and the goal for each year is $100m. If the revenue of AAV increases $100m in year one, is the strategy working and has it been adopted? Most will say yes. Be careful. If the results of the strategy are better than expected in one section yet worse in another, it is not an indication of general adoption.

## Summary

The structural connection pinpoints the detailed behavior the strategy calls for throughout the organization. This connection facilitates the discovery process where the organization identifies the strategy-related behavioral change requirements. The connection promotes collaboration and engagement of everyone impacted by the strategy to ensure the new actions are well aligned with the new strategy.

The structural connection also delineates the day-to-day operational actions from strategy-related actions. This separation is fundamental to the creation of this connection and the development of the contractual connection, described in the next chapter. It is not only the separation of the actions but the alignment of the new actions with the strategy that is important.

The structural connection also addresses the issue of reconciliation. It breaks the organization's goals down to the individual level and ensures that the individual is clear regarding his or her personal performance requirements. The connection reconciles those personal commitments with the overall goals, resulting in realistic expectations.

The process of creating the structural connection and the deliverables are critical to the development of the contractual connection. It is of utmost importance to develop and refine this connection in detail.

## CHAPTER FIVE

# Contractual Connection

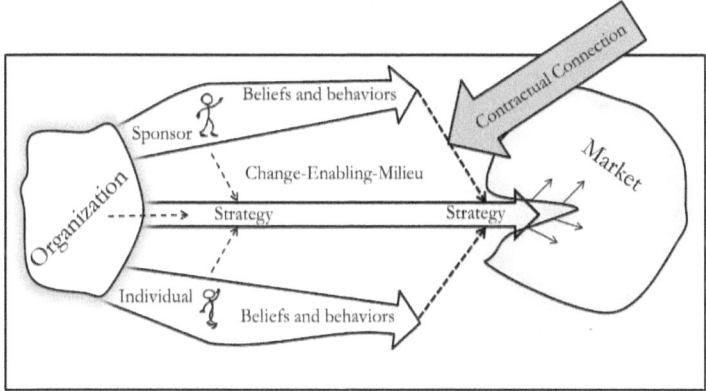

*Figure 5.1. The Contractual Connection in Strategy Implementation*

## The Critical Connections

- *Psychological* connection unlocks individuals' willingness to change their behavior.

- *Structural* connection pinpoints the detailed behavior changes the strategy calls for throughout the organization

- *Contractual* connection anchors and lock individuals' new negotiated behavior.

# Why Is a Contractual Connection Important?

The organization is on a journey, moving between the old strategy and the new. The psychological connection has unlocked the impacted individuals' willingness to review their transactional agreements with the organization. Through the structural connection, the individuals and the organization defined the behavior that aligns with the new strategy. This will allow the organization to penetrate the market space as designed. The contractual connection anchors and locks down the newly aligned behaviors through new behavioral contracts. The commitment by individuals is to adopt those behaviors that align with the new strategy.

The creation of the contractual agreement is so fundamental to strategy implementation that, without it, individuals will not engage in the new behavior, or over time will revert back to their old behaviors. Both actions have dire consequences for the new strategy.

At this stage, the impacted individuals are aware of the needed changes, have agreed to them, and in collaboration with their sponsors have set performance standards. The stage is now set to document the changes and develop the new contractual agreements with every individual in the organization. The strategy is activated, and the organization is now moving in the newly designed direction.

# Transform Theory to Practice

The contractual connection captures all the new changes the strategy calls for in new job descriptions, performance reviews, targets, and reward agreements. These changes take effect on a specific date, which becomes the official transition from the old to the new strategy. We can therefore argue that the contractual connection transforms the conceptual and theoretical plans into action.

**Align recognition** Recognition for performance is inherent to the contractual connection. "You get what you reward," according to LeBoeuf (LeBoeuf, 1986). This concept is critical to the success of the strategy and one of its main drivers. Just imagine what would happen if Tom Black's (the sales rep in the hypothetical Phoenix office) annual performance review was still based on the old strategy's metrics, yet the organization expected him to embrace the changes associated with the new strategy. This inherent misalignment between performance management and newly aligned behaviors the new strategy calls for would be cancer to any strategy.

**Promote sustainability** Once the behavior is locked in through the job description and performance management system, it becomes the default behavior that increases the sustainability of the strategy. Most individuals prefer stability over instability. It took the development of a psychological connection to unlock their willingness to engage in negotiating new behaviors. It will take the development of another psychological connection to make another round of behavioral changes once the new behaviors are securely locked in through the contractual connection. If the new behaviors are not locked in, individuals will revert back to the old generic job performance expectations.

**Enable accountability** The contractual connection sets the stage for the organization to hold individuals accountable for their actions. Setting the stage and putting the mechanisms in place is a first step toward holding people accountable, although it does not ensure accountability. Whether organizations keep individuals accountable for their actions depends on the sponsors' willingness to act. Many well-intended and well-designed strategies fail at this point. The organization may have done all it takes to be successful, but if the organization and sponsors hesitate to hold people accountable, they can undo the strategy.

**Link individual actions to operational needs** An important aspect of the contractual connection is that it links the individual's behavior to the operational needs. This may seem insignificant, but let's look at it through the lens of a sponsor. Job descriptions are traditionally managed by the HR department with little or no reference to strategy. This defect is one of the main reasons new strategies fail. The contractual connection enables the development of an individual's job description with a dual function. It sets baseline performance expectations and links to a future new strategy. Both elements are important to the success of the strategy.

## Why the Contractual Connection Is Traditionally Not Created

Despite the obvious importance of the structural connection, it is often omitted in strategy development and implementation for a variety of reasons.

**HR Function** Job descriptions, performance reviews, and recognition are traditionally handled by HR. HR's well-defined role and responsibility in the organization is traditionally more focused on the legal compliance side of the employer/employee relations than on strategy. The results are that most job descriptions focus on functionality only. I've reviewed many job descriptions and found little or no mention of specific strategy-aligned behavior. HR traditionally focuses on job parity and role definition than on promoting a specific strategy.

**Cultural** Organizational culture develops over time. If an organization developed a specific practice to design job descriptions and link that to a traditional performance review process, it becomes challenging to change. Individuals are sensitive to what they need to do and how they are assessed and compensated. This is linked to the psychological contract between the individual and the organization where the individual is recruited, retained, and rewarded based on a professional class reflected in the job description. Changing that elephant in the room requires significant sponsorship. In most cases there will be unwillingness from HR to embrace the recommended change. Therefore, most of the organizations will not consider changing the way they manage job descriptions and performance reviews.

**Unions** Collective bargaining is fundamentally focused on functionality and contracts that stretch over several years. Unions are important stakeholders and should be engaged in the process. Most union leaders we encountered were receptive to the idea that there is a clear differentiation between the baseline expectations and strategy-related expectations.

**Time factor** The perception that it will take a lot of time and resources to change a large amount of job descriptions discourages organizations from making the necessary changes. It is important to overcome this natural obstacle. There is already a contractual connection in organizations. Most of the time may not be aligned with the current strategy and can, in fact, be totally disconnected from any strategy. This unstructured connection is a main driver of failing strategies and when left unchanged will hamper the implementation of a new strategy. Allocating the time to create the contractual connection is fundamental to the success of the new strategy and should therefore not be avoided.

**Perception of complexity** Reviewing and changing most of the job descriptions in an organization is not easily accomplished but can be done. Organizations may have many excuses for not creating the necessary contractual connection. Resource load and time consumption are most often blamed.

We have also seen organizations leverage technology and internal collaboration sites to develop a system where the job description management by HR is much more dynamic. Those organizations are able to create the contractual connections without hesitation.

## Creating a Contractual Connection

Creating a contractual connection will anchor and lock in the negotiated behaviors. Redesigning the job descriptions, performance appraisals, and rewards and recognition systems are required to create the contractual connection.

The challenge is to overcome the resistance and create it in efficient, effective ways to ensure the strategy's sustainability. Here are some suggestions:

**Design "smart" job descriptions** A "smart" job description describes both professional expectations as well as strategy related expectations. It enables the organization to have a clearly defined contract with an individual that elevates the focus on functionality and strategy at the same time. How is the new job description different from what exists today? The new job description combines baseline expectations with individual strategy-aligned action steps (more information to follow).

**Baseline expectations in a job description** "Kathy Cook" at AAV Pharmaceuticals is the marketing manager in the local Phoenix office. From a traditional perspective, the baseline expectation for her position is to be a professional marketing manager and to:

- manage and coordinate all marketing, advertising, and promotional staff and activities;

- conduct market research to determine market requirements for existing and future products;

- analyze customer research, current market conditions, and competitor information;

- develop and implement marketing plans and projects for new and existing products;

- manage the productivity of the marketing plans and projects;

- monitor, review, and report on all marketing activity and results;
- determine and manage the marketing budget;
- deliver marketing activity within agreed budget;
- develop pricing strategy; and
- liaison with media and advertising.

Most organizations recognize the importance of clearly defined baseline expectations for each role in the organization. These are the minimum expectations for each position and individuals in those positions. For Kathy Cook, this means the organization expects her to execute on every expectation and deliver the contracted services of the expected standard.

Kathy knew what these expectations were before she accepted this position. She had more than one opportunity to clarify the expectations and confirmed, through her signature, that she will provide the services as specified. These expectations are also aligned with Kathy's identity as marketing manager and her psychological contract with the organization where she is willing to provide certain services in return for compensation and career opportunities. Making changes to the baseline expectations requires thoughtfulness from the organization's side. Organizations cannot just arbitrarily change baseline expectations without the consent of the impacted individual.

The baseline expectations also introduce a level of standardization in the organization. It sets the stage for developing similar expectations for all people in similar positions and promotes job or position comparison, even with similar positions outside the organization. This is a healthy practice, done well by HR, and ensures competitive compensation for similar positions in the market. In most organizations these are the only explicit expectations. There might be other expectations, but the formalized expectations are the ones the individual sees as critical to his or her relationship with the organization.

**Strategy-aligned responsibilities** Inserting the individual's strategy-aligned action steps into the job description is paramount to creating the contractual connection. This step in the process will only be meaningful if the psychological and structural connections were created and the changed behavior is delivering the expected results.

The main output of the structural connection is the detailed, negotiated strategy-aligned action steps. Every individual will have a different set of negotiated actions that need to be captured in the contractual agreement. There can be no generalization of professional class or job level. Every individual will take responsibility for delivering the agreed-upon goals within the set time frame.

This step anchors the discussion, and support for the new strategy is locked in with the performance review and compensation discussion that follows. These action steps should lead to the discussion of goal-related rewards or consequence.

Lets look briefly at the actions steps Kathy Cook (marketing manager in the local Phoenix office) agreed to with the implementation of the new strategy

- Target A and B food and pharmacy stores and develop them as clients of AAV Pharmaceuticals.

- Conduct four demonstrations at the local Z food stores.

- Target and develop D store in Prescott as a client.

- Target and develop E store in Yuma as a client.

- Increase marketing of nonprescription drugs at all current and new clients.

- Sponsor the Little League tournament at Goodyear.

- Implement the new research database on all local laptops.

- Identify new prospective clients using the new research tool.

- Conduct presentations of AAV Pharmaceuticals's products at local venues in the state.

- Distribute the new marketing materials at the local food stores.

- Increase customer satisfaction scores from 6.7 to 7.7 during this year.

Note that the actions steps Kathy agreed to are directly aligned with the main strategic drivers. There is an underlying assumption that if Kathy delivers on the action steps and meets or exceeds the success metrics, her contribution will move the organization forward in the direction of the new strategy. It is also important to recognize that if Kathy only focuses on the baseline expectations, the strategy will not get the support needed to move forward.

The development of the smart job description will bring two worlds together. A smart job description combines skills, competencies, and strategy-aligned expectations into a single format. It creates the professional world of the individual, a person trained and educated to deliver a specific service for the organization as well as the world of the organization, where the strategic goal is to penetrate selected market space in order to provide a positive return to investors and/or owners.

The creation of the contractual connection is dependent on the creation of the psychological and structural connection. As stated earlier, the psychological connection unlocks individuals' willingness to negotiate a different contract with his or her employer. That willingness should translate into the newly designed job description.

The following pages show the traditional job description of a marketing manager, and although the content is abbreviated, the gist of it reflects job descriptions currently used in many organizations. Following that is a revised version. The differences should be noticeable. The new job description links the individual action steps directly to the strategy and captures the agreed-upon goals, and its content flows seamlessly into the next segment of the connection, the performance review. If this step is done well, the next step is a smooth continuation.

*Table 5.2. Traditional Job Description*

**Traditional Job Description**

**MARKETING MANAGER**

To develop, establish, and maintain marketing strategies to meet organizational objectives. Effective management of the marketing, advertising, and promotional activities of the organization.

**Main Tasks and Responsibilities:**
- Manage and coordinate all marketing, advertising, and promotional staff and activities
- Conduct market research to determine market requirements for existing and future products
- Analysis of customer research, current market conditions, and competitor information
- Develop and implement marketing plans and projects for new and existing products
- Manage the productivity of the marketing plans and projects
- Monitor, review, and report on all marketing activity and results
- Determine and manage the marketing budget
- Deliver marketing activity within agreed budget
- Develop pricing strategy
- Liaison with media and advertising

**Key Competencies:**
- Excellent written and verbal communication skills
- Organization and planning
- Problem analysis and problem solving
- Team leadership
- Formal presentation skills
- Persuasiveness
- Adaptability
- Innovation
- Judgment
- Decision making
- Stress tolerance
- Collaboration

*Table 5.3. Strategy-Aligned Job Description*

(Note: the baseline expectations and basic competencies have been excluded in this example. The reason is these elements are relatively standard and defined by an organization's needs. The differences we wanted to point to are the changes related to the alignment to the strategy. The individual action steps are directly related to the strategy and defined in measurable terms and specific goals.)

| MARKETING MANAGER (Kathy Cook) | | |
|---|---|---|
| To develop, establish, and maintain marketing strategies to meet organizational objectives. Effective management of the marketing, advertising, and promotional activities of the organization | | |
| **(Expectations)** | | |
| **(Competencies)** | | |
| **Strategic Drivers** | **Personal Action Steps** | **Goals** |
| Target biggest food retail stores | • Target A and B food and drug stores and develop them as clients of AAV Pharmaceuticals <br><br> • Conduct four demonstrations at the local Z food stores | • Increase sales revenue by $200k <br><br> • Add two additional clients in Phoenix |
| Expand the west coast region | • Target and develop D store in Prescott as a client. <br><br> • Target and develop E store in Yuma as a client | • Add one additional client outside Phoenix |

| Focus on nonprescription drugs | • Increase marketing of nonprescription drugs at all current and new clients<br>• Sponsor the Little League tournament at Goodyear | • Increase name recognition in Phoenix from 3.4 to 5.5 on the survey |
|---|---|---|
| Leverage new technology | • Implement the new research database on all local laptops.<br>• Identify new prospective clients using the new research tool. | • Migrate from old research tools to the new tool |
| Promote brand | • Do presentations of our products at local venues in the state.<br>• Distribute the new marketing materials at the local food stores. | • Conduct ten presentation throughout the state |
| Distinctive client service | • Increase customer satisfaction score from 6.7 to 7.7 out of 10 during this year. | • Customer satisfaction score of 7.7/10 |

The structural connection pinpoints the detailed behavior changes the strategy calls for throughout the organization. The detailed changes are reflected in individual job descriptions. On the other hand, the psychological connection unlocks the individuals' willingness to identify the needed changes and negotiate how it will be executed. These connections pave the way for the development of an individual's new action items, captured in a new job description. Embed action items from the job description into the business plans. It is now time for reconciliation. In this step, the individual job descriptions' content is transcribed into the local office's business plans.

We have already looked at the new job description of Kathy Cook, the marketing manager in the Phoenix office. Let's look at it from the local office's perspective, using one of the strategic drivers. At the local office level are six individuals—five marketing staff and the office manager—impacted by the strategic driver.

In the next graphic, the local office consolidated the actions steps supporting strategy driver one (target biggest food and drug stores) in the business plan. It lists all employees involved. It also provides the detail actions each person agreed to focus on, complemented by everybody's specific goal.

*Table 5.4. Consolidated Job Description*

(Note: Only the strategy-related information is consolidated. This enables local store members to see who is actually responsible for which goals.)

| Phoenix Office (Three-Year Goals) (Cindy Smith) | | |
|---|---|---|
| **Employee** | **Target Biggest Food and Drug Retail Stores** | **Goals** |
| Kathy Cook | • Target A and B food and drug stores and develop them as clients<br>• Conduct four demonstrations at the local Z health food store | • Increase sales revenue by $200k<br>• Add two additional clients in Phoenix and Prescott |
| Jane Moore | • Target K and M food and drug stores and develop them as clients<br>• Invite managers from E and F stores to our annual banquet | • Increase sales revenue by $150k<br>• Add two additional clients in Phoenix |
| Pete Good | • Target G and H food and drug stores and develop them as clients<br>• Arrange with the local TV stations for a morning interview and talk about our new over-the-counter meds | • Increase sales revenue by $100k<br>• Add two additional clients in Phoenix |
| Tom Black | • Target I and J food and drug stores and develop them as clients<br>• Host two chamber-of-commerce events | • Increase sales revenue by $200k<br>• Add two additional clients in Phoenix and Yuma |

113

| Sandy Depp | • Target K food and drug store and develop them as clients<br><br>• Target the health spa in Phoenix as potential client<br><br>• Sponsor two CEO breakfast meetings in Phoenix | • Increase sales revenue by $50k |
|---|---|---|
| Phoenix office | • Consolidate actions for strategy driver one | • Increase sales revenue by $700k<br><br>• Add eight additional clients in Phoenix and SW Arizona |

There are several advantages to this process:

- Transparency is a critical element in developing trust and strengthening the psychological connection. Consolidating all contributions into a visible business plan builds trust.

- Fairness is fundamental to the relationship between employers and employees. The new business plan points out that the responsibility for making the strategy work is shared. The specific targets or goals negotiated and committed to are based on the individual's specific work circumstances. For example, Tom Black may have a big account while Sandy Depp has smaller accounts. Tom Black, therefore, gets a more robust target.

- Mutual accountability is promoted. Every person in the office knows what the others are expected to accomplish, and they can support each other.

- Teamwork is promoted. As we see in the diagram, the office has a collective goal, and this goal may be accomplished even if one person does not make the expected individual goals. It is a matter of teamwork where the weakest performer can be helped by the stronger performers.

The manager is responsible for the office's performance, which is the cumulative efforts of every impacted individual.

The importance of the psychological and structural connections should be clear at this time. The manager is also an individual affected by the change in strategy. She needs to be open and willing to negotiate her own new behaviors with her sponsor before she can become a sponsor to her direct reports. If the psychological and structural connections have not been made with the manager, she will not take responsibility to support the process for her direct reports. It is critical that the process cascades down the authority lines in the organization so the manager can be fully engaged in designing the action steps and defining the expected outcomes.

It is of utmost importance that the manager is personally engaged in the process and that she has developed a high level of confidence in the probability that the intended results can and will be achieved. These point to one of the main reasons most strategies fail: individuals are not fully engaged in defining their aligned actions and intended results. If an individual fails, he or she blames management for "unrealistic goals." This blame game is cancerous to any strategy.

It is clear that the manager agreed to the action steps and set goals. The manager is willing to take full responsibility for achieving the intended results.

The given example also points to the fact that reconciliation is developed from the lowest level to the highest in the organization. Cindy Smith, the local office manager in the Phoenix store is willing to accept responsibility to grow the revenue by $700k over the next three years and has a high level of confidence that it will be realized.

It is also important to note that during the original top-down cascading process, the executives allocated a revenue growth of one million dollars to the local Phoenix office. They did the allocation based on the information they had at the time without knowing the realities at the local level. As the local office manager, Cindy Smith, has the responsibility to take the given guidelines, translate the intent to the local individuals, and combine the local market realities with her direct reports' abilities and skills to reach a reasonable workable solution. In the above example, the local office committed to a seven hundred thousand dollar revenue increase and to securing eight more clients in their market.

The reconciliation of the actions from the lowest level to the top of the organization enables the executives to adjust their expectations but also to feel more confident that the intended results can be realized. The executives have to adjust the Phoenix office's revenue increase from one million to seven hundred thousand. Achieving this point in the process opens the door for the next critical step, namely, performance review.

## Align Performance Reviews With Individual Job Descriptions

The next step in creating the contractual connection is to link the individual performance review process to the job description. This is the last key step in establishing the connection and should conclude the negotiations.

Cindy Smith was fully engaged and worked collaboratively with her direct reports in the Phoenix office designing achievable, strategy-aligned action steps during the contractual connection phase. Before the new strategy is activated, Cindy needs to feel comfortable with the performance-review process and potential outcomes. The final stage of the negotiations is to lock in and anchor the performance-review process and documentation, as we see in the next diagram.

Let's point to a few aspects in the next diagram, the performance-review document.

- The strategy drivers and negotiated actions and goals are transferred from the job description changes and are still in alignment with the strategy as well as the local office's business plan.

- The performance criteria are added to the mix. Although this is just an example, note that every organization has a blend of performance criteria with elements that have worked well for them in the past. Every organization should customize this portion of the process to fit its culture and history. Changing this process on the fly is not a good idea and will fuel a tremendous amount of unwarranted resistance that may derail the work done to date.

- The calculation or scoring of the results is customized to the organization.

- The allocations of increases to compensation or bonuses are organization based.

- The individual is compensated for achieving strategic goals through an annual bonus. The individual earns a salary for meeting baseline expectations. There may be an annual salary increase for exceeding baseline expectations.

- It is also the privilege of the organization to value selected actions more than others. In this example, the organization allocated a premium on the revenue growth strategic drives to ensure that it got the needed attention to realize the expected results.

116

*Table 5.5. Strategy-Aligned Job Performance Review*

**Cindy Smith's performance review at the end of the first year**

| Cindy Smith, Office Manager in the Phoenix Store | | | |
|---|---|---|---|
| **Annual Performance Review** | | | |
| **Strategic Drivers** | **Personal Action Steps** | **Goals** | **Performance** |
| Target biggest food and drug retail stores | • Target A and B food and drug stores and develop them as clients of AAV Pharmaceuticals<br><br>• Conduct four demonstrations at the local Z food stores | • Increase sales revenue by $50k<br><br>• Add 2 additional clients in Phoenix | Underperform<br>Meet<br>Exceed<br>1 2 3 4 **5** x2 |
| Expand the west coast region | • Target and develop D store in Prescott as a client.<br><br>• Target and develop E store in Yuma as a client | • Add one additional client outside Phoenix | Underperform<br>Meet<br>Exceed<br>1 **2** 3 4 5 |
| Focus on non-prescription drugs | • Increase marketing of nonprescription drugs at all the current and new clients<br><br>• Sponsor the Little League Tournament at Goodyear | • Increase name recognition in Phoenix from 3.4 to 5.5 | Underperform<br>Meet<br>Exceed<br>1 **2** 3 4 5 |
| Leverage new technology | • Implement the new research database on all local laptops.<br><br>• Identify new prospective clients using the new research tool. | • Migrate from old research tools to the new tool | Underperform<br>Meet<br>Exceed<br>1 **2** 3 4 5 |

| Promote brand | • Do presentations of our products at local venues in the state.<br><br>• Distribute the new marketing materials at the local food stores. | • Conduct ten presentations in the state | Underperform<br>Meet<br>Exceed<br>1 2 3 4 5 |
|---|---|---|---|
| Distinctive client service | • Increase your customer satisfaction score from 6.7 to 7.7 during this year. | • Client satisfaction score of 7.7 | Underperform<br>Meet<br>Exceed<br>1 2 3 4 5 |
| **Baseline Expectations (360 assessment)** | | | Underperform<br>Meet<br>Exceed<br>4.7 |
| **Comments: Cindy did a great job given the challenges in the local economy. Cindy qualifies for the pay increase and an annual bonus of $8,000.** | | | **Final Score**<br>**31/40** |

## *Align Policies and Procedures*

The final action in creating the contractual connection is the alignment of all impacted policies and procedures. It is true that not all policies and procedures will need to be changed. However, not changing them has a negative impact on the contractual connection. People are held accountable for acting within the set boundaries, and if they notice differences between the organizational policies and procedures and the newly negotiated changes, they will hesitate to act and effectively hold off on making any personal commitments and/or changes.

Let's look at a few policies and procedures that will most likely change.

Most organizations have policies and procedures related to performance reviews and/or job descriptions. As organizations make changes to their performance review processes, policies will need to be reviewed to determine whether changes are needed.

Organizations have specific policies and procedures related to the business planning process. As we made changes to the business-planning process during the creation of the structural connection, these policies should be reviewed to ensure a sound reflection of the process changes.

Recruiting is impacted by the creation of the three new connections. Prospective employees should be aware that the organization is integrating the core strategy into individual job descriptions and that new recruits will be held responsible for the strategy. Setting accurate expectations is critical to prospective employees. Aligning the applicable policies and procedures is important to the successful creation of the contractual connection.

The uniqueness of each organization warrants that they screen all policies and procedures during the development and implementation of a new strategy. Engaging those impacted individuals in the process will reinforce the executives' commitment to the change and will send a sound and powerful message.

Once the contractual connection has been made, a new question comes to the fore: How can an organization ensure the newly created connection will stay intact and effective?

## *Sustaining a Contractual Connection*

The contractual connection is created to anchor the new strategy in a contractual arrangement between the organization and all impacted employees. This is accomplished through adjusting the individual job descriptions and aligning the organization's performance-review process with the strategy and the actions of the individual.

How do we sustain the connection?

**Frequent review** Critical to the success of the contractual connection is frequent assessment of progress. Should an organization create a contractual connection and not revisit it until the next annual review, the connection and its created advantages will be lost.

The strategy unfolds over time. Tom Black, the Phoenix office sales rep, needs to add two additional clients to his portfolio, and that will not happen on day one. It is also unwise to wait until the last day of the year to realize that Tom is going to miss his goals. It is of utmost importance to do regular progress reviews. What is the ideal frequency? Progress may not be visible in increments as small as monthly reviews. Most organizations seem to benefit from quarterly reviews. There are a few goals that can only be measured annually. In those cases, it becomes important to determine the best estimates.

**Incremental adjustments** In a transactional relationship between the individual and the organization, incremental adjustment is critical to sustaining the contractual connection. AAV Pharmaceuticals keeps the local office manager accountable for an increase in revenue of $700k. It is important for the manager to keep track of his direct reports' progress and to share it with the organization. A healthy relationship between the individual and the organization exists when both are agreeable to adjust goals if and when needed.

What happens if the local office manager increases his office's revenue within six months to $1.2M, significantly exceeding the goal? In this situation the organization should adjust the Phoenix office's goal, as well as the goals of the employees in the office. Updating the local goals will enable the adjustment of the organization's goal during a revised reconciliation. The adjusted values will enable executives to adjust their goals and set new expectations. The adjustment will also allow the executives to provide more accurate revenue forecasts to the shareholders and/or analysts.

One significant advantage of incremental adjustments is continued engagement between individuals and the organization. These interactions strengthen the contractual connection and significantly improve the effectiveness of the connection. Subsequently, it keeps the strategy on the radar.

**Agreed-upon consequences** Successful strategies are invariably intertwined with real consequences, positive and negative. The purpose of the contractual connection is to lock in and anchor the strategy. The locking mechanism is critical to the success of the strategy. It is vital to the connection that the consequences are mutually accepted before being instituted.

Tom Black, in AAV Pharmaceuticals's Phoenix office, agreed he will deliver specific results as it relates to the new strategy: (1) he will increase his revenue $200K for the firm, and (2) he will add an additional two big clients to his list, thus increasing market share.

Tom and AAV Pharmaceuticals also agreed that if he succeeds, the organization will (1) allocate his annual standard pay raise, and (2) give him an $8k bonus if he meets his goals plus $15k if he exceeds his revenue goal by more than 20 percent. Tom had a clear understanding of his expectations, and AAV Pharmaceuticals knew how to reward him.

The question is not what will happen should he meet or exceed his goals but what will happen if he misses them. Once again, Tom and AAV Pharmaceuticals reached an understanding during the negotiations that (1) if Tom misses the goals he will not qualify for a bonus, and (2) if he only maintains current levels of revenue and client count—in other words, does little or nothing to move the strategy forward—he risks being put on probation.

Tom realized the risk and asked to have quarterly reviews to keep the organization well-informed of his progress and avoid any surprises. The regular updates give AAV Pharmaceuticals the opportunity to change Tom's support system and help him succeed. It also gives Tom's peers the opportunity to assist him if he needs it. Transparency is fundamental in the alignment of rewards and recognition.

The bigger question is whether organizations will stick to their plans as they relate to rewards. An organization may spend time and resources developing a change-enabling milieu and the three critical connections, sustain them for a year, and then undo all the work by rewarding individuals outside the scope of the agreements.

Many organizations have an internal culture where they find it not only challenging but impossible not to give annual pay raises to every person regardless of performance. When individuals underperform, they are often reassigned by the organization to a different department without any real consequences.

Organizations have conflicting needs: (1) developing and implementing a new strategy linked to consequences, and (2) keeping the morale high by providing increases and bonuses to all. These conflicting needs are extremely dangerous to strategy implementations, and approaching it more holistically will elevate these conflicting needs and give the organization the opportunity to align them.

Executives have the final word in the development and implementation of the strategy. They can choose to execute the strategy as implemented, applying all the rewards and consequences and becoming successful. Or they can choose to deviate, effectively undoing the new strategy, and fail. The principle—that you get what you reward—stands. The organization covered a great deal of ground developing and implementing a new strategy, just to kill it themselves by rewarding misaligned behavior. The choice is clear. At the end of the day it boils down to this: Can an executive take strategic concepts, share them with others through engagement, unlock their willingness to change, collaboratively identify the detailed behavior changes needed, reach agreement to new performance standards, and persevere until the strategy produces the expected results?

## *The Strength of the Contractual Connection*

The strength of the contractual connection is determined by the thoroughness of the administrative process, quality of the content, and disciplined execution of the plan.

Organizations have internal processes to develop and approve job descriptions. These functions are traditionally housed in HR and can be either partially or fully automated. For organizations with fully automated processes, the alignment of all the job descriptions as well as the performance reviews are less problematic.

The quality of the content is determined by the level of details collaboratively defined and the development of the performance measurements. Clear quantitative performance measures increase the organization's ability to manage accountability.

Acting in accordance with the agreements is vital to the strength of the contractual connection. What good is it to have a contract that nobody enforces? Who of us will pay our insurance premiums diligently if the insurer does not cover our damages? Similarly, who of us will pay attention to a job description if the organization rewards individuals because they are well-liked rather than based on performance?

A strategy comes to fruition when it is well-designed, when all impacted individuals are engaged, and when it is anchored in the job descriptions and performance reviews, as well as when both parties live up to the agreements.

## *Identifying a Weak Contractual Connection*

There are several clear indicators that point to a weakening contractual connection. The key is in finding the soft spots early and deploying mitigation actions. If left unattended, the connection will break, detaching the impacted individuals from the strategy, which will result in the partial or complete failure of the strategy. Let's explore some of the key indicators pointing to a weak or weakening contractual connection.

**Job descriptions are baseline driven:** The first and most obvious indication of a weak contractual connection will be reflected in the job descriptions. A random sample of job descriptions will point to the fact that the strategy is not embedded in individual job descriptions. This is a basic violation of the principle "you get what you reward." The lack of reference in the job-description design of the strategy is a clear indication that the organization has either not developed a contractual connection or has not closed the loops on the required actions.

**Action steps are ambiguous:** Actions are not functionally designed. Ambiguity in a job description is cancerous to strategy. An individual needs to know exactly what is expected of him or her and what behaviors will lead to success before a contractual connection will succeed. When organizations look at their employees' job descriptions, they find references similar to (1) continuing serving clients; (2) providing good client service; (3) promoting name brand recognition; and (4) communicating effectively through the job descriptions. These may be great statements but are ambiguous and do not mean anything in a contract because they are not measurable.

**No measurements link to actions:** Imagine driving with a car without instruments. How many people will buy a vehicle that was designed without instruments indicating speed or fuel level? The driver has been given no information. Would you take your family on a coast-to-coast trip in a vehicle like this? Why do organizations allocate so many resources to implement a strategy without measurements? Not seeing measurements in job descriptions is a clear indication of a weak contractual connection.

**Qualitative over quantitative measures:** Organizations must maintain a balance between qualitative and quantitative measures for the individuals' action steps, which can be a challenge. A contractual connection is stronger when the actions are described in specific terms, such as "improve client satisfaction from 6 to 7," rather than in evasive language like "deliver distinctive client services." The less the measurements are specified, the weaker the connection.

**No regularly scheduled review:** Any contractual connection will deteriorate when organizations do not have a regular review process. Organizations are unique and should establish their own review frequency. Most organizations find quarterly reviews effective.

**No regularly scheduled adjustments:** A regularly scheduled review of the strategy's performance—based on individual performances—should translate to adjusting performance expectations. A red flag is raised when organizations do not have regular performance adjustments. Most organizations will argue that they do. However, that information is based on overall data and can seldom be traced to the individual level, making it challenging to take effective action.

**The performance review process is detached from the strategy:** It is driven by baseline expectations only. As stated earlier, the contractual connection serves to anchor the strategy to the individual through accountability. When an assessment of the performance review process finds a disconnect between rewards and strategy, it points to a flaw. If this is left unattended, it will suffocate the strategy.

**No consequences related to missed goals:** Rewarding individuals for misaligned or general baseline performance at the cost of the strategy is an indication of a weak contractual connection. The weakness is detected by reviewing the executives' bonus recommendations. When the recommendation is inconsistent with the contractual connection agreements, it weakens the contractual connection.

**A lack of transparency:** One of the strengths of the integrated approach to the development and implementation of a strategy is transparency. It builds trust and distributes the risk or weight more evenly throughout organizations. Lack of or limited transparency is a clear sign of a weak contractual connection.

**Inconsistent accountability:** Inconsistent accountability is apparent in many organizations. One section of the organization will enforce the contractual agreements and another will abandon it, for whatever reason. Those sections that do not abide by the contractual agreements create a tidal wave that will hit the rest of the organization with a shock, resulting in most sections abandoning the contractual connection. The reason for this is that it is much easier to be nice to employees that to be just to them. Inconsistent accountability should be avoided, because correcting it is not only challenging but nearly impossible. "All for one and one for all" is the secret to success.

**Weakening sponsorship:** Supporting sponsors may abandon the contractual agreement or parts thereof, and in doing so they weaken the connection, which can lead to its collapse. The best result comes from unity, and any exceptions to the approach will not only weaken the connection but threaten it.

Organizations can deploy relatively inexpensive but effective mechanisms in detecting weaknesses. A document review will uncover a weak contractual connection and will point to the underlying causes of the aforementioned issues.

## Repair a Weak Contractual Connection

Prevention is more effective and time-saving than cure. Repairing a weak contractual connection is challenging but possible. Restoring a collapsed connection will consume a terrific amount of resources. The key message is that creating the contractual connection will anchor the strategy and significantly increase the odds of success. Neglecting the maintenance of the connection will lead to a trust violation between the leadership and employees, jeopardizing the success of the strategy.

If the contractual connection is weakening, where should the organization focus their recovery efforts?

The number one reason for a weakening contractual connection is sponsorship. The recovery effort should primarily focus on sponsorship. There are three critical messages to share with all the sponsors: (1) the short-term consequences; (3) the long-term consequences; and (3) that the details related to a weakening connection is inconsistent accountability (as described in the previous section).

The recovery process is activated by sharing the details related to the detected weakness. As mentioned earlier, transparency is paramount to the success of the strategy. It is therefore necessary to share the information openly, seeing that the failure of the connection on one side of the organization will lead to a failure on the other side.

The contractual connection links all impacted individuals. Every individual has accepted a responsibility toward making a contribution to the success of the strategy. When everyone is successful, funds will be available to meet all the contractual arrangements such as bonuses or salary increases. The failure of the connection in one area of the organization may limit that area's ability to uphold all the agreements, so transparency is important to the recovery process.

Elevate the short-term consequences and ensure all the sponsors are aware of the details. Some of the most frequent short-term consequences are dissatisfaction among individuals and the departure of some high-performing individuals. The reaction over the short term sounds manageable and creates the illusion that the organization will overcome it, and the strategy will be successful. Remember, a tsunami is barely noticeable in the open waters. In the same way, a short-term reaction sounds insignificant, but if left unchecked will surprise the sponsors, managers, and leaders in the organization.

The long-term implications are that the strategy will fail, adding all the ramifications associated with it, and there will be a lack of trust in the organization. There is no question in my mind that the executives will be held responsible for a failed strategy. Evidence to that effect is visible all over the business landscape. The lack of trust will impede the executives in introducing another strategy. This problem is traditionally overcome by replacing key executives.

The power to repair the contractual connection is in the hands of the executives and supporting sponsors. When they become aware that the contractual connection is at risk, they have a choice to make: either fix the problem, or become part of the statistics related to failed strategies.

## Summary

A new strategy calls for a new set of behaviors with the goal to bring about improved or specific results. The development and introduction of new individual behaviors leads to instability, change, and transition. The contractual connection stabilizes the organization by anchoring the strategy at the individual level. This relative stable internal time provides the new set of behaviors the environment needed to deliver the anticipated and designed results.

The contractual connection is the final phase in transforming the strategy from basic concepts to measurable action steps at the individual level. It serves as the foundation of accountability, a critical aspect of a successful strategy implementation.

Creating the contractual connection is a challenging task for most organizations. Culture and well-established internal processes in developing job descriptions and performance reviews drive an organizations' hesitation to engage in this critical step. Despite the inherent difficulties, the risks and consequences of not creating contractual connections far outweigh the effort in developing them.

When organizations embrace the value of the contractual connection and change internal processes to create it, they receive the additional benefit of organizational nimbleness. When an organization is successful in creating one, it also enables them to accelerate future change implementations.

The contractual connection clarifies the individual's and organization's strategy-related responsibilities. The impacted individuals become fully aware of their responsibilities, as the actions steps are captured in their job descriptions. They develop a sound understanding of the organization's expectations and have clarity related to the consequences if expectations are not met. The organization has the responsibility for rewarding those individuals who make or exceed expectations and administer consequences to those who do not.

All parties need to live up to all the agreements in order for the strategy to succeed. The psychological and structural connections pave the way for the contractual connection, but the strategy can only come to fruition once the contractual connection has been forged.

# Conclusion

Precious time and resources are consumed by failed strategy implementations. The reality is that most strategy implementations fail or never produce their intended results. In a time when every dime counts, with increased market pressures and competition, it is a business imperative to rethink the way organizational strategies are developed and implemented. Our conclusions, based on practical experience, strive to provide guidelines regarding the way strategy can be implemented in the most expedient effective manner, increasing an organization's ability to be successful.

Strategic changes are driven by a desire to improve or change business/financial results. A strategy change necessitates a complex, comprehensive set of sustained individual behavior changes and should be managed accordingly. As such, strategy selection, as well as strategy implementation requires thoughtfulness, thoroughness, and a detailed plan to drive the adoption. Every time an organization changes strategy, it calls for a new, specific set of individual behavioral changes and requires a deliberate effort to move individuals to a point where they adopt the behavior changes, creating alignment between the strategy and the organization.

The projected results of the strategy have to be measurable, so an organization can conclude whether the strategy is indeed delivering the intended results. A return on investment (ROI) is based on the organization's ability to measure the impact of the strategy. Successful organizations know it is best to measure the impact of the strategy at various levels, as positive preliminary results from one area do not necessarily mean the strategy has been adopted throughout the organization or is successful overall.

A strategy's results are dependent upon the quality of the solution and the level of adoption. Because a strategy change calls for a behavior change, individuals' adoption of new behaviors is fundamental to its success. The level of adoption is directly related to the performance of the strategy. To focus only on the quality of the solution/strategy and not focus on the adoption is to leave 50 percent of the strategy unattended. A relatively weak but well-adopted strategy will outperform a strong strategy that is poorly adopted. It is a business imperative to drive adoption as hard as you drive the creation of the solution.

Behavior change is linked to the individual's willingness to change. The organization needs to focus on unlocking the individual's willingness. If it is not addressed, it will put the adoption of the strategy at risk, because people will either not change at all or will change for a while and then revert back to previous behavior. The mechanism to unlock this willingness to change is made through the psychological connection.

An individual's commitment to change is also related to his or her perception of the impact of the change at the personal level. Organizations have to engage all impacted individuals to uncover the detailed actions they will have to execute for the strategy to be successful and to support everyone in the transition. The structural connection, in combination with the psychological connection, facilitates this process.

All changes take place within a specific organizational milieu, which consists of culture, history, trust, and expectations. For adoption to occur and the strategy to be successful, the organizational milieu has to be deliberately assessed and architected to become a change-enabling milieu. This requires that all aspects of the current milieu need to be assessed to determine the degree to which they will either enable or inhibit change. Deficiencies need to be addressed proactively in order for the environment to become a change-enabling milieu.

Culture is one of the critical elements in a change-enabling milieu. Culture is a broad concept, and when a strategy changes only the specific cultural elements that may stand in the way, the strategy needs to be addressed and managed. The specific cultural beliefs and behaviors that may stand in the way of adoption need to be assessed, validated, exposed, and changed.

The organization's change-related history is another critical element in a change-enabling milieu. The changing environment requires a perpetual organizational change in order to be successful. Organizations build a change history. A positive history can benefit strategy implementation, and executives can create a strong association between the current implementation and previous successes. However, if there is a perception of failed strategy implementations, the current implementation will be sluggish and at risk.

Executives can minimize the impact of the negative history by clearly distinguishing between the current implementation and past failures. It is important that executives do not make assumptions about how the history is perceived, as the perceptions may differ significantly at different levels. Assessing the perception of the history is fundamental in the development of a change-enabling milieu.

Trust is the next critical element. If individuals have trust in their leader or the solution, people will be more willing to change their behavior. A lack of trust drives resistance-related behavior. The level of trust varies significantly throughout the organization. It is therefore imperative that trust needs to be assessed throughout the organization to ensure that pockets of limited trust are addressed.

In a change-enabling milieu, expectations are addressed and managed. Meeting or exceeding expectations enhance trust in the organization. The first challenge is determining what individuals' expectations are. Organizations seldom focus on expectations because they don't realize the significant impact it will have on the change-enabling milieu. They also don't realize that expectations can vary significantly throughout the organization. Without assessing expectations, the organization may create expectancy and trust violations that will hamper the adoption of new behavior. Expectations need to be managed to ensure that violations do not occur and to enhance people's willingness to adopt the new strategy-aligned behavior.

In the hand of the sponsor, communication is the primary tool for driving change. Individuals need specific, sequential information to unlock their willingness and move them from a state of unawareness to adoption. The sponsor uses communication to provide this sequenced information to meet the needs of the impacted individuals. When used effectively, it creates a change-enabling milieu that promotes the adoption of a new strategy.

Sponsorship is the most critical element in a change-enabling milieu. It legitimizes change in an organization, and without strong sponsorship change is unlikely to occur, or if any change occurs, it will not be sustainable. Sponsors cannot delegate the responsibilities related to strategy change and need to be held accountable for the implementation and execution of the strategy. Effective sponsorship significantly enhances the change-enabling milieu.

Sponsorship is a subset of management in that it coordinates activities, allocates resources, manages schedules and holds people accountable. It is not synonymous with leadership. It focuses on developing the change-enabling milieu and the three critical connections between the strategy and the impacted individuals. Where management focuses on the current day-to-day operations, sponsorship focuses on the design and building of future operations. As it becomes operational, the supporting function is transferred back to management.

Experience alone does not guarantee effective sponsorship. Sponsorship training will increase sponsors' ability to provide effective services for the duration of the implementation. Organizations will benefit by well-designed sponsorship training.

Effective sponsorship is crucial in unlocking an individual's willingness to adopt new behaviors. Sponsorship is a personal service to direct reports. It is crucial that sponsors have a clear understanding of their role and responsibilities in providing the service. Direct reports need their sponsor's support during the transition from the current strategy to the new.

Sponsors are the conduits in cascading the strategy and related information to all impacted individuals. This crucial role necessitates the development of sponsorship down to the lowest level in the organization. Contrary to popular belief, the quality of sponsorship may differ vastly throughout the organization, putting the implementation at risk. It is imperative for sponsorship to be assessed at all levels. Organizations should strive to develop homogeneous sponsorship and monitor the quality throughout the life cycle of the strategy. They should address weaknesses as soon as they are detected.

In terms of implementing the strategy, sponsors are responsible for the business side and the individuals in the organization. A successful strategy pivots on the sponsors' ability to meet the organization's needs and the needs of the individuals in a fair and balanced way. This balance needs to be maintained while creating the three critical connections.

Strategy adoption is dependent on the creation of three critical connections between the strategy and those impacted. This pivots on the organization's ability to identify and create the psychological, structural, and contractual connections and maintain them for the lifetime of the strategy. A disconnect of any of these connections at any time will not only jeopardize the implementation, it will put the whole strategy at risk. The three critical connections need to be developed from the start to secure a successful implementation.

Organizations tend to focus more on establishing the psychological connection, are somewhat reluctant to build a structural connection, and seldom attend to the contractual connection. However, the consequence of not paying attention to all three connections results in a high strategy failure rate. Organizations will significantly enhance their ability to implement a strategy if they invest equally in building and maintaining all three connections.

A significant amount of behavior change can be orchestrated by changing a specific key belief, because beliefs drive behavior. Once a belief is changed, the behavior change becomes sustainable. It is a great investment of time and resources to uncover the few critical beliefs underpinning the new strategy and to devise a plan to alter any opposing beliefs. Getting people to move out of their comfort zones is not easy.

The psychological connection unlocks individuals' willingness to move out of their comfort zone by experimenting with and adopting new aligned behavior. Organizations can coerce individuals to change, but at the first possible opportunity they will revert back to their old behavior, causing the strategy to fail. The psychological connection meets the individual's need for the specific sequenced information, which enables them to voluntarily adopt the new behaviors. Organizations have the responsibility to provide this information and should deliberately shape and design their communication plan to meet the needs of the individual. A misaligned communication plan can be extremely hazardous to this process. If the organization executes on its responsibility to satisfy individuals' needs during a transition, the result is a sustainable change and a successful strategy implementation.

Through the structural connection, the sponsors and their direct reports uncover the detailed, measurable behavior changes the strategy calls for throughout the organization. This detailed information provides clarity and specificity to the individuals, enhancing their willingness to embrace new behaviors. The structural connection also clarifies how realistic the strategic goals are. It reconciles the commitment at the individual level with the expectations at the organizational level. This connection is embedded in the business-planning process and provides the opportunity to cascade the strategy from the top to the lowest level of the organization. It is this aligned behavior that significantly enhances the ability of the organization to bring the strategy to fruition. Most strategies are reflected in high-level business plans, yet a successful implementation demands that the strategy be reflected down to the individual level.

The contractual connection anchors and locks in the individuals' newly negotiated behavior, capturing and documenting it and creating the mechanism to hold the individual accountable for such behavior. A high degree of collaboration and engagement is needed to create the contractual connection where the individual willingly agrees to be held accountable for these documented changes. Without this connection, there is a high probability that an organization will move in one direction and the strategy in another. The contractual connection aligns the individual behavior with the strategy, enabling the realization.

The contractual connection manifests in individual job descriptions, performance management, and rewards systems. Senior executives are able to assess the level of traction a strategy has gained in an organization by reviewing individual job descriptions and performance reviews. The more evidence there is that the strategy is fully articulated at the individual level the higher the probability of success. This is one of the most significant validation points for gaining insight to the degree that the strategy has been embedded into the organization.

Sustainability of the strategy is dependent upon the maintenance of the contractual connection. If the organization does not act on the agreements reached in the contractual connection, such as providing rewards or consequences, it will create a trust and expectancy violation. These violations alter the change-enabling milieu into a change-inhibiting milieu, which can quickly derail the strategy.

Organizations need to monitor the strength of the connections throughout the life cycle of the strategy. It is dangerous to assume that once a connection has been created the environment will remain stable through the implementation of the strategy. Change-enabling milieus are dynamic, and the critical connections are fragile. A constant monitoring of the milieu and the connections are critical to ensure the strategy's success.

The cost associated with the proactive maintenance of the milieu and the connections are significantly lower than reactive repair. Repairing any one of these connections or the change-enabling milieu significantly delays implementation.

A strategy needs time to mature in order to provide the opportunity to realize the results. It is analogous to the act of pruning a grapevine in order to bring about a better harvest the following season. Once the pruning is completed, the vine is watered, fertilized, and monitored until it brings about the results. In the same way, once a strategy has been implemented it needs to be maintained and allowed to mature in order to bring about the intended results.

Organizations often fail to fully implement a strategy to the individual level and then feel compelled to keep changing the strategy. In order to have a successful strategy, the organization needs to plan and execute a detailed, thoughtful implementation plan, and once it is implemented, the strategy should be given the opportunity to yield the intended results.

Sponsors can undo strategies. The minute the sponsor does not provide the sponsoring service to his or her direct reports the implementation comes to a standstill. Should the sponsor decide to focus his attention elsewhere and sponsor different actions, it unravels the strategy and causes it to fail. It is critical for them to understand the impact of their actions on the adoption of the strategy. The undoing can happen intentionally or unintentionally and should always be monitored.

Executive leaders design strategic concepts; however, they need to be translated into action steps that can be cascaded throughout the organization. It is their responsibility to direct this translation and monitor the alignment down to the individual level in order to assess the level of adoption throughout the organization. Executive leaders' visible support for the strategy is critical as it instills and builds trust among those impacted. This trust will enhance their willingness to adopt new behaviors. Impacted individuals observe their leaders closely, and once they see a discrepancy between their words and actions, their willingness to embrace the new strategy will be compromised.

Accountability is fundamental to a strategy's success. Regardless of whether the connections have been made down to the lowest level, if the sponsors are unwilling or unable to hold their direct reports accountable, the strategy will be undone. Without accountability, strategies fail.

Designing accountability is only the first step. The second is the willingness and ability on the organization's side to hold people accountable for their strategy-related actions or lack thereof.

Alignment between the strategy and individual actions is fundamental to the success of the strategy. The results of the cumulative aligned actions of all impacted individuals bring the strategy to fruition. The organization should put forth significant effort to ensure alignment between the strategy and an individual's actions. Any deviating actions will significantly weaken the strategy's ability to realize the intended result. Unity is power, and alignment creates the unity.

In this competitive environment, organizations cannot risk partially successful or failed strategy implementations. By creating a change-enabling milieu and the three critical connections, they can significantly increase their chances of organization-wide adoption of strategy-aligned behavior. Given that the success of a strategy is contingent on the quality of the solution and the adoption, organizations will become more successful if they pay equal attention to strategy design and its implementation. The benefits of a successful implementation allow the organization to rival its competitors and attract investments and the best talent, whereby satisfying all shareholders.

# About the Author

**ALBERT VERMEULEN** is the president of Arrowhead Management & Associates LLC, a consulting firm that specializes in driving the adoption of corporate strategies in collaboration with organizational leaders. He participated in the political transformation in South Africa (1986–1995) and gained valuable insight into how the people impacted by the transformation adopted new concepts, beliefs, and behavior. He also developed an in-depth understanding of the psychological impact on people when they are exposed to small or significant change.

Since 1996 Albert has worked and researched in the United States. He introduces organizations to the concepts and supports the creation of the psychological, structural, and contractual connections needed to secure the adoption of corporate strategies in order for them to yield the expected results. He has supported numerous large organizations in managing strategy development and implementations as well as associated organizational change initiatives. Health care, public accounting, pharmaceutical, manufacturing, and technology are some of the industries he has consulted with. Albert has a special interest in professional services firms.

He spends his time coaching, consulting, and training organizational leaders as they develop and implement new strategies. His ability to balance theory and practice enables him to drive accelerated strategy adoption. Albert is a Purdue graduate and lives in Phoenix, Arizona.

# Glossary

Change-enabling milieu: An organizational milieu that facilitates and sustains the implementation of change.

Psychological connection: The connection that unlocks an individual's willingness to change their behavior.

Collaboration site: An electronic workspace that multiple people have access to and where they can simultaneously interact with one another and the content.

Sponsorship: One who assumes responsibility for someone or something.

Contractual connection: The connection that anchors and locks individual's new negotiated behavior.

Gate: The gate is a small addition to the business-planning process, where the owners of the sub-business plans have to present them to senior leadership, demonstrating how their plans align with the new strategy.

Silo: An organizational group that is working in isolation, not collaborating with adjacent groups to achieve collaborative results.

Smart job descriptions: A "smart" job description describes both professional expectations as well as strategy related expectations. It enables the organization to have a clearly defined contract with an individual that elevates the focus on functionality and strategy at the same time.

Structural connection: The connection that pinpoints the detailed behavioral changes the strategy calls for throughout the organization.

# Bibliography

Conner, D. R. (2006). *Managing at the Seed of Change* . New York: Random House.

Covey, S. (2006). *The 7 Habits of Highly Effective People.* Free Press.

Schein, E. H. (1997). Organizational Culture & Leadership?

Kralewski, J. E., et al. (2008 Sep–Oct). Culture as a Management Tool for Medical Groups. *Physician Exec*, 34(5):12–4, 16–8.

LeBoeuf, M. (1986). *How to Motivate People: Reward, The Greatest Management Principle in the World.* Letchworth: Mankiins, M. C., & Steele, R. (January 2006). The Garden City Press.

Mankins, M. C., & Steele, R. (2006, Jan ). Stop Making Plans; Start Making Decisions. *Harvard Business Review.*

Nelson (2010) *Managing for Dummies, 3rd Edition*, chapter 21, page 325.

Tway, D. C. (1993). A Construct of Trust. Dissertation.

# Index

*illus* indicates an illustration

## A

AAV Pharmaceutical (hypothetical organization)
  adjustments in transactional relationship, 120
  agreed-upon consequences, 120–121
  assessment of progress, 119
  business plan, 113–114
  business-planning process, 8
  cascading, 86–87
  communicating and communication, 42, 44–45
  corporate strategy, 90 *illus*
  individual (personal) action steps, 93 *illus*
  job descriptions, 105–106, 107, 110–111
  performance reviews, 100, 102, 116, 117
  reconciliation, 115
  review of structure connection, 99
  strategy action steps, 92 *illus*
  strategy drivers, 91 *illus*
  success metrics, 87–88, 96, 97
abilities
  and adoption of new behavior, 20, 27, 67
  of executives, 48
acceptance, "false" signal of, 18

accountability, 9, 55, 95–96, 103, 114, 122, 124–126, 135
action steps
  adjustment of, 98
  cascading, 94, 96
  consequences of ambiguous action steps, 123
  design of, 115
  drivers as translated into, 8, 86–87
  individual (personal) action steps, 93 *illus*, 105, 106, 108, 110, 117, 123
  and job descriptions, 110–111
  measurability of, 97
  measures for, 123, 126
  monitoring of, 97
  and rewards and consequences, 107
  strategy action steps, 92 *illus*
  strategy as translated into, 87–88, 90–94, 135
  weaknesses in, 123
adaptation capacity, 88
adoption
  of behavior changes, importance of, 5–6
  as dependent upon, 132
  as one of eight steps in change process, 67–69, 69 *illus*, 79–80
  quality of, 11–12, 61, 129–130
agreed-upon consequences, 95, 120–121, 134
alignment
  of behavior with new strategy, 23

www.ingramcontent.com/pod-product-compliance
Lightning Source LLC
Chambersburg PA
CBHW032017170526
45157CB00002B/737